A Circle in the Square

Rabbi Shlomo Riskin
Reinvents the Synagogue

A CIRCLE IN THE SQUARE

RABBI SHLOMO RISKIN
REINVENTS THE SYNAGOGUE

BY EDWARD ABRAMSON

URIM PUBLICATIONS
Jerusalem • New York

A Circle in the Square: Rabbi Shlomo Riskin Reinvents the Synagogue
By Edward Abramson
Copyright © 2008 by Edward Abramson

Printed at Hemed Press, Israel. First Edition.
Layout design by Satya Levine.

ISBN 978-965-524-014-6

Urim Publications
P.O. Box 52287, Jerusalem 91521 Israel

Lambda Publishers Inc.
527 Empire Blvd., Brooklyn, New York 11225 U.S.A.
Tel: 718-972-5449 Fax: 718-972-6307, mh@ejudaica.com

www.UrimPublications.com

To Dorona, Dov, and Elie

שלי ושלכם שלו הוא

I wanted everything to belong to me, for all that beauty to be a part of what I was, and I remember trying to remember it, trying to store it up for later, trying to hold on to it for a time when I would really need it…. The things themselves passed too quickly…. The only thing that remains for me is a blur, a bright and beautiful blur….

– Paul Auster, *In the Country of Last Things*

CONTENTS

ACKNOWLEDGMENTS

IN THEIR ACKNOWLEDGMENTS, writers typically express gratitude to individuals who have assisted them specifically with their projects. However, in the spirit of Jewish tradition, I would like to begin by acknowledging people from my past. I thank – *in absentia,* sadly – my parents, Anne and Bert Abramson, who against all odds raised me as a searching Jew in the very non-Jewish environment of Watertown, New York. My father died suddenly two months before my bar mitzvah, and I acknowledge him even as I still search for him. The short notes of love and encouragement he left for me inside many of the Jewish books in our home continue to fuel my search. Some years later, my mother made the amazing transition from small-town storekeeper to woman-about-Manhattan, lending her spirit, humor, and life-force to the building of Lincoln Square Synagogue.

A Circle in the Square would never have come to fruition without Keren Keshet – The Rainbow Foundation and the insight of its trustees, Mem Bernstein and Arthur Fried. Not only did Keshet provide a generous grant which enabled the research and writing of this book, but Mem, Arthur, and Linda Sakacs of the Foundation offered their encouragement and guidance along every step of the way. There is a beautiful thread here, because Mem's late husband, Zalman C. Bernstein, may his memory serve as a blessing, inspired by Rabbi Riskin, dedicated so much of his time and boundless energy to infusing the world of the Jewish spirit with the same verve and excellence with which he imbued his professional life.

The leaders of North America's Modern Orthodox community-at-large helped me explore the effect of Rabbi Riskin's tenure at Lincoln Square on Modern Orthodox Judaism. I would like to thank in particular Richard Joel, President of Yeshiva University, Rabbi Kenneth Brander, Dean of the

Center for the Jewish Future of that institution, and Rabbi Avi Weiss, Founder and Dean of Yeshivat Chovevei Torah for their time and invaluable perspective.

My research was significantly aided by the help of Shulamith Z. Berger, Curator of Special Collections at the Yeshiva University Library, who allowed me the use of library's archives.

Thanks to Ellen Freudenheim Wiener for her invaluable help.

Jeffrey Gurock, Professor of History at Yeshiva University, Professor Samuel Heilman of Queens College, noted sociologist and ethnographer of the Orthodox Jewish community, and Jenna Weissman Joselit, Professor of Jewish History at Princeton University, all offered me encouragement in writing this book. Since I am neither a sociologist nor a historian, their belief in the project helped me immeasurably.

Thanks to Joe Blank, Executive Director of Lincoln Square Synagogue, and to his office staff for giving me access to the synagogue's archives, and to long-time LSS members Rachel Herlands and Rose Landowne for locating material in those archives.

Of course, without the "Lincoln Square people"– those individuals who experienced the LSS "magic" first-hand – there would be no book. Thanks to the current leaders of Lincoln Square Synagogue: Rabbi Shaul Robinson, Cantor Sherwood Goffin, and Rabbi Ephraim Buchwald. I would especially like to thank Shulie Cohen for sharing her memories of her husband, our dear friend, Rabbi Herschel Cohen, may his memory serve as a blessing.

I am extremely grateful to the following people – many of them close friends of mine from the Lincoln Square days – who allowed themselves to be interviewed and shared their experiences and recollections in order to help me create this book: Peter and Debbie Abelow, Amos and Miryam Alter, Bob and Lissa Bernat, Dr. Robert Bersson, Daniel Besdin, Rabbi Jack Bieler, Freda Birnbaum, Jack and Lenore Brown, Jesse Cogan, Rabbi Edward and Meira Davis, Fred Ehrman, Muk Eisenmann, Stanley and Phyllis Getzler, Fred and Chaya Gorsetman, Richard Joselit, Aron and Edith Landau, Morton and Rose Landowne, Danny Mars-Margolis and Emma Mars, Leonid (Aryeh) Rigerman, Maurice and Marian Spanbock, Steven

Spira, William Stanley, Dr. Roy and Judi Stern, Rudy Treitel, Joel Wachs, and Mark and Shirley Wald.

Rabbi Shlomo Riskin, my spiritual mentor and *rebbe*, set aside many hours that his pressured schedule really did not permit in order to sit with me and be interviewed for this book. While *A Circle in the Square* is filled with words about Rabbi Riskin, they are woefully insufficient in conveying who he really is. Rabbi Riskin's sense of urgency about what must be done for the spiritual welfare of the Jewish people and for the world-at-large is so strong that he does not allow himself to become easily distracted. I have so many things for which to be grateful to him, but I will limit myself to thanking him for his willingness to reflect on his time at Lincoln Square Synagogue for the purpose of this book. Thanks also to Vicky Riskin for her unique insights into her husband's special qualities, and her detailed recollections of the very early days.

To my editor, Sorelle Weinstein, no amount of thanks is sufficient. Her questions were the right questions even when they were not easy to answer. Her organizational ability, her facility with the English language, and her insistence on follow-through created a book out of a manuscript. Her real contribution, however, came out of a deep and fresh understanding of my words and ideas, and the intellectual and spiritual vigor to make sense out of them. If there are errors, they are mine. If the reader has clarity of understanding, thanks go to Sorelle.

To "acknowledge" the help of my wife, Miriam, in the writing of this book would be to trivialize her contribution. For the last thirty-eight years, our shared vision has been to live the Lincoln Square message, which has made our Judaism sing and has inspired our children Dorona, Dov, and Elie, to whom this book is dedicated.

INTRODUCTION

I HAD THE GREAT PRIVILEGE of attending Lincoln Square Synagogue (LSS) in its early years, from 1967 to 1973, before I was ordained myself. Those years at LSS were in many ways the most valuable of my life. I met my wife Miriam at LSS, my mother renewed her life there, and I received the unofficial rabbinic apprenticeship of a lifetime.

I was motivated to write *A Circle in the Square* after a nostalgic conversation on Purim night in 2004 with my friend Aryeh Shiran from Kibbutz Lavi. Stirred by the joy of the evening and talk of *kiruv* (outreach to Jews who lack Jewish background), I reminisced about "the old days at Lincoln Square." As I was talking, it struck me how fascinating those times were, and as a result, I was inspired to write this book.

The story that I tell is full of contradictions and dissonance. It tells of a very young rabbi teaching an ancient religion; it describes an urban synagogue in a secular city; and it delivers the ultimate surprise: Jews with no Jewish background come together to experience God. In *A Circle in the Square*, I demonstrate how Rabbi Riskin caused American Jews from across the spectrum to become impassioned about Judaism, to embrace its rituals, and to adhere to its ethics and values.

In Part One, Sowing the Seeds, I examine the three components that set the stage for the birth and growth of Lincoln Square Synagogue. In Chapter One, I analyze the strong societal currents of the 1960s and 1970s and demonstrate how many of these trends related to the dynamics within LSS. It is important to note that the history of Lincoln Square Synagogue is not covered by a discussion of the history of Jewish Orthodoxy in America or the history of Orthodox synagogues in New York. Lincoln Square Synagogue began as a Conservative synagogue and, under Rabbi Riskin, became an Orthodox one, but neither of those rubrics sufficiently defines or describes this unusual place.

Locus is a significant factor in all human affairs, and Manhattan's West Side presented a set of factors and complexities which I believe significantly affected Lincoln Square's founding and development. Chapter Two deals with the transformative power of a new upscale, culturally-enriched neighborhood redeemed from the edge of Hell's Kitchen, a district in Manhattan formerly noted for its slums and vice. This chapter suggests a connection between the re-make of the Lincoln Square geographical area and the re-creation of Jewish lives within the Lincoln Square Synagogue community.

Of course, this story is about Rabbi Riskin himself. In Chapter Three, I dig deeply to find out who Rabbi Riskin was as a human being, and explore how his personal history and childhood shaped his thinking and attitudes toward religion and humankind.

The heart of this book is an exploration of Lincoln Square's message. In Part Two, I examine the message of Lincoln Square Synagogue, which was deeply embedded in a series of programs, events, sermons, classes and discussions. I also thought it important to try to understand from the Lincoln Square congregants what they saw as the major themes of the rabbi's presentations. From both of these perspectives, I try to show what was new and different here and how the community became so deeply infused with the message that was being taught.

In order to understand the message, I break it down into its component parts. How did Rabbi Riskin end up as rabbi of Lincoln Square Synagogue at the age of twenty-three? It was never Steven Riskin's plan to become a pulpit rabbi. He favored the idea of teaching in an academic setting. Chapter Four tells the story of Lincoln Square Synagogue's search for a rabbi for the High Holidays and Yeshiva University's recruitment of Rabbi Riskin for the position.

One might assume that after Rabbi Riskin's success in convincing his secular congregants to install a *mechitza* – a physical partition separating the sexes during prayer – he would have been eager to identify his synagogue as belonging to the Orthodox stream. This was not the case. In Chapter Five, I describe how only a year after he assumed the pulpit, Rabbi Riskin announced in an article entitled "Our Credo" that the synagogue was disregarding "the usual labels of Orthodox, Conservative, and Reform in order to create a Spiritual Center rooted in the eternal truths of the Jewish Law." This document acted as a catalyst for spiritual growth and commitment to Jewish law without the restrictive elements that accompany labels.

In Chapter Six, I reveal how Rabbi Riskin revolutionized the previously moribund area of adult Jewish education. When Rabbi Riskin assumed the pulpit of Lincoln Square Synagogue, his congregants were not looking to express their Jewish identity through Torah study. However, Rabbi Riskin strongly believed that he could not encourage his congregants to adopt a religiously observant lifestyle without first teaching them central Jewish concepts and texts. He made Jewish learning so stimulating and engrossing that his congregants and members of the general public who attended his lectures could not wait until their next encounter with him to be challenged even more.

It was one thing to teach ideas, even complex ideas, to those with a limited background in Judaism. It was quite another matter to teach faith. In Rabbi Riskin's mind, without faith the Bible becomes "ancient mythology and the Talmud a branch of logic." In Chapter Seven, I explore Rabbi Riskin's approach to prayer as a means of creating a spiritual environment within the synagogue.

How do you teach the beauty and spirit of the Sabbath to people who have never before experienced it and who are unaware of its significance? Chapter Eight discusses Rabbi Riskin's unflinching commitment to making Shabbat – not just the synagogue services – the center of his congregation's life.

I devote Chapter Nine to Rabbi Riskin's attitude towards the role of women in Judaism. When Rabbi Riskin joined Lincoln Square Synagogue, the status of women in Judaism had just begun to become a topic of debate, particularly in Orthodox Judaism. I describe how Rabbi Riskin repeatedly emphasized the equality of the sexes before God and demonstrated that the roles of men and women could be equal in worth, but different in practice.

Chapter Ten describes how Rabbi Riskin's boundless energy impelled him to reach outward, beyond the four walls of his synagogue. He truly believed that Torah was for everyone, not just for those who chose to be involved with Lincoln Square Synagogue. The concept of Jewish outreach in the 1960s and 1970s was extremely unpopular, and aside from the Lubavitch movement, which also believed in spreading Jewish observance beyond the already-committed religious community, no movement existed to acquaint unaffiliated Jews with their Judaism. In the eyes of most people, reaching out beyond one's community of Jews to other Jews was equivalent to proselytizing. I demonstrate in this chapter that Rabbi Riskin's vision of moving out of the synagogue to Jews on the street shattered the popular notion that a spiritual leader had to wait for people to find the synagogue.

In Chapter Eleven, which I have called "God as a Guest in the Synagogue," I deal with the spirituality that everyone in the 1960s was seeking and still seeks today. Rabbi Riskin restored a sense of mystery to religion and brought his congregants close enough to experience that mystery. This chapter has to do with Rabbi Riskin introducing God to his congregants and students as a Friend, as a Parent, as a Mate. It has everything to do with raising a synagogue, even a monumentally successful synagogue, one more step – to the level of a shrine, an altar, a holy mountain.

Finally, what does it all mean, and where has it gone? Was there a permanent legacy from the "Riskin years" at Lincoln Square Synagogue? What can be learned from Rabbi Riskin's brand of Jewish outreach that we can use today? These are the questions that occupy Chapter Twelve, the book's conclusion.

But we are far away from that conclusion, and much needs to be felt, experienced, and understood in order to get there. So we begin the journey with a trip back in time in order to follow our small group of Manhattan Jews and their new rabbi.

PROLOGUE

DANNY MARS WAS WORRIED. It was spring of 1964, and his small group of Manhattan Jews had a problem. Rosh Hashana was just months away and they had no rabbi. Last year's rabbi had done well, but this year he wanted a "larger honorarium," as he put it, and there was no way this group would come up with that kind of money.

After all, it was not as if their informal get-togethers, which were mainly of a social nature, required the services of a rabbi. They were simply a group of secular Jews who believed it was a good thing for Jewish people to get together and enjoy each other's company. Besides, they all lived in the same building – 303 West 66th Street. But for the High Holidays, you needed a rabbi.

The founder of this group, Danny Mars, wasn't religiously observant, but an incident that had occurred just two years before on Yom Kippur acted as an impetus for the founding of the prayer group. Danny woke up on Yom Kippur morning in 1962 with the realization that he had to find a synagogue where he could say *Yizkor* (the prayer for departed souls recited in every synagogue and temple as part of the Yom Kippur service) for his father, who had passed away just a year before. But which synagogue? Danny suggested to his wife Emma that they go down the street to Congregation Habonim, a venerable Reform Temple which had opened its new building on West 66th Street just a few years before.

Danny and Emma arrived at Habonim's door, ready to proceed to their seats. Rather naively, Danny and Emma assumed that any Jew who shows up at a synagogue or Temple on Yom Kippur would be ushered in immediately. A somewhat overzealous usher at Habonim felt otherwise. "Your tickets, sir." Danny quietly informed the gentleman that he and

Emma had no tickets; they just wanted to pray. The usher then uttered the words that, perhaps more than any other statement from an outside source, led to the founding of Lincoln Square Synagogue: "Sorry sir, I cannot admit you without tickets."

Danny recalls feeling disappointment, then anger. "All right," he responded. "I'll start my own synagogue and we won't ever stop anyone from coming in, tickets or no tickets!" Danny kept his promise to the usher; he started his own synagogue. He gathered together a group of about thirty Jewish people who lived in his building. This group put up posters publicizing the services and scoured the area in search of Jews who had no synagogue affiliation but who wanted a place to pray on the holidays. They even searched through a reverse telephone directory, which enabled them to search by address rather than name, and contacted those people whose surnames sounded Jewish.

The group succeeded in attracting almost two hundred people to their first service, which took place on Rosh Hashana of 1963 in the rented ballroom of the Esplanade Hotel on West End Avenue and 74th Street. Danny Mars's new synagogue was starting to take off.

In the following year, 1964, Danny Mars' group was faced with a problem. The rabbi from the Conservative Jewish Theological Seminary who had led the High Holiday services last year had been good, but now he wanted double the money. Danny discussed the situation with Sidney Trompeter, who was the most knowledgeable about Judaism of all the members. Sidney suggested they contact Yeshiva University (YU). Perhaps one of their rabbis would be willing to accept a smaller sum. Although Danny was strongly against the idea of hiring an Orthodox rabbi, he agreed to contact Yeshiva University.

Dr. Samuel Belkin of blessed memory, President of Yeshiva University, was well aware that Orthodox Judaism in America was in a state of crisis. The Conservative Movement was gaining fast, and American Jews were opting in droves to affiliate with Conservative synagogues. It was difficult to

17

shake off the image of Orthodoxy as being old-fashioned and out of touch with American society. True, Yeshiva University was still ordaining young rabbis. But what good were rabbis if there were no pulpits for them, and even if there were pulpits available, would the synagogues maintain the standards of Jewish Orthodoxy? Belkin knew what he must do if Orthodox Judaism was to continue to exist on American soil: he had to select young and dynamic rabbis and place them in synagogues.

As soon as Dr. Belkin received the call from Danny Mars's group, he knew which rabbi he would send them. The members of this group were not particularly observant and were unsure of what they wanted out of a synagogue or a rabbi. They needed someone bright, intellectual, and energetic; a person who could give respect as well as command it, and a rabbi who would inspire them to grow in their Judaism. He would send them the newly-ordained Rabbi Steven Riskin.

PART ONE

SOWING THE SEEDS

❧ 1 ❧

THE TIME

IN 1964, THE YEAR THAT RABBI RISKIN assumed the pulpit at Lincoln Square Synagogue, religion in America seemed to be thriving.[1] Statistics showed an increase in church and synagogue construction and in church attendance at that time. Religious holidays were being celebrated and priests, rabbis, and ministers delivered sermons in which they related Biblical texts and principles of faith to current events.

To the sensitive observer, however, religion was in a state of crisis. The cataclysmic events of the 1960s were too frightening to be explained by the tools of religion, namely faith and good works. In 1963, President Kennedy – that charismatic promise-maker of a New Frontier – had been assassinated, and no one knew why or, with any certainty, by whom. The Vietnam War was raging with no end in sight. Kitty Genovese, a New York woman, was stabbed to death near her home. According to public perception at the time, her thirty-eight neighbors passively watched the murder take place from their windows, not one of them coming to her aid.

Religion knew what its role was supposed to be – to answer the questions about what was happening – but so many of those answers were radical, too. In the midst of this turbulent decade, a new theology arose: "the death of God." On April 8, 1966, the cover of *Time* Magazine shouted in huge red letters the following question: "Is God Dead?" The cover story explained that although polls showed that church attendance was on the rise,

---

[1] Mark Oppenheimer, *Knocking on Heaven's Door: American Religion in the Age of Counterculture*. New Haven: Yale University Press, 2003, 8.

and that 97 percent of Americans held a belief in God, "a small band of radical theologians has seriously argued that the churches must accept the fact of God's death, and get along without him."[2] It wasn't so much a question of the size of this "small band" of theologians; what was significant was the fact that God's existence was now fair game for discussion and debate, even among those committed to religion. This debate signaled yet another upheaval in the fabric of American society during the sixties.

The "God is dead" theologians insisted that religion could exist without God. One of the central voices of this movement, theology professor Gabriel Vahanian, explained that:

> [A person's] religiosity is no longer shaped by the idea that God is the precondition of man. Other norms govern this religiosity. One could characterize it by saying, in general terms, that where it was once heteronomous now it is autonomous; where it was once theocentric now it is anthropocentric; where it was transcendental it is now immanentist.[3]

The question "Is God dead?" did not exist in a vacuum. A year before the publication of the *Time* magazine article, Divinity Professor Harvey Cox of Harvard had published *The Secular City*, which examined the thesis of religion in an era of secularization. Cox, in a book which ultimately sold over one million copies, told us that:

> The age of the secular city, the epoch whose ethos is quickly spreading to every corner of the globe, is an age of "no religion at all." It no longer looks to religious rules and rituals for its morality or its meanings....[4]

---

[2] "Toward a Hidden God." *Time*, April 8, 1966.

[3] Gabriel Vahanian, *God and Utopia: The Church in a Technological Civilization*. New York: The Seabury Press, 1977, 11.

[4] Harvey Cox, *The Secular City: Secularization and Urbanization in Theological Perspective*. New York: The Macmillan Company, 1965, 3.

Although Cox did not group himself with the "God is dead" theologians, there was clearly a connection between the secularization process that he described and the perception that God was no longer a significant factor in human affairs.

Although the influence of religion had certainly not disappeared from the United States by 1964, it was becoming increasingly difficult to see its relevance. In 1964, blacks and whites were clashing violently in the United States. In June of that year, three civil rights volunteers, two from New York and the third an African-American from Mississippi, were murdered in Mississippi while working in support of civil rights. In the second half of 1964, the center of the conflict moved from the South to major Northeast cities, where numerous riots took place. Many had the sense that the very thread of American society was unraveling and that nothing could stop the downward spiral.

One would think that religion could have played a healing role here, and many figures – the Reverend Martin Luther King most prominent among them – tried to use religion to heal the rift between the two sides. On the whole, however, their efforts failed. Each side of the conflict claimed that God and religion supported its view, and so, to a great extent, the effect of religion in this crisis was neutralized.[5]

In response to the failures of organized religion, the counterculture movement during the sixties was very strong, and this decade saw a significant increase in the number of religious communes. Although there was a strong religious impulse during the sixties, most of the cultural changes that this impulse occasioned were impermanent and given to failure.[6] The religious communes' attempt to emphasize spirituality and to create a sense

---

[5] Charles Marsh, *God's Long Summer: Stories of Faith and Civil Rights.* Princeton, New Jersey: Princeton University Press, 1997, 3.

[6] Camille Paglia, "Cults and Cosmic Consciousness: Religious Vision in the American 1960s." *Arion: A Journal of Humanities and the Classics* 10/3 (Winter 2003): 63. This is an expanded version of a lecture delivered on March 26, 2002 at Yale University, sponsored by the Institute for the Advanced Study of Religion at Yale.

of community around God often degenerated into widespread drug use and free sex. Ironically,

> the most important changes came in old, traditional denominations, not in sects, cults, communes, or movements from the East. Most new religious movements had few adherents and shrank quickly or even disappeared. Few adherents of the new religions were still devoted, regular practitioners a decade or two later.... The counterculture changed American religion through its insinuations into traditional denominations....[7]

So it was in the general community. Established religion came under fire during a period of great societal upheaval. Religious experimentation abounded but generally succeeded only in producing further alienation and disappointment. Against this background of general social and religious unrest, American Jews experienced their own religious crisis. How similar was their particular Jewish experience to the experience of the population of the United States as a whole?

Jews of America

For the Jews, it was the same, but different. In the 1960s, the Eastern-European Jewish presence in the United States had reached its third generation. While the first two generations had experienced tremendous conflict between their Judaism and their place in American society, the third generation was unburdened by such dilemmas. Will Herberg, writing in 1960, wrote:

> The third generation... felt secure in its American-ness, and therefore no longer saw any reason for the attitude of rejection so characteristic of its predecessors.[8]

---

[7] Oppenheimer, *Knocking on Heaven's Door,* 2.

[8] Will Herberg, *Protestant, Catholic, Jew: An Essay in American Religious Sociology.* Garden City, New York: Doubleday & Company, 1960, 189.

Herberg also cited a then-unpublished survey by sociologist and primary Jewish chronicler of the time, Marshall Sklare, in which

> Fully 97 per cent of the [Jewish] adolescents [in an eastern seaboard city with a Jewish population of 8,500], when asked, "What is a Jew," replied in terms of religion, as against 80 per cent of the parents.[9]

Herberg commented, "with self-identification in religious terms almost universal among American Jews… synagogue affiliation grew markedly in the decade after World War II."[10]

In fact, the period which began after World War II and continued into the 1960s was marked by what many observers called a "Jewish revival." Historian Jonathan B. Sarna characterizes American Jews' renewed interest in their Jewish identity as manifesting itself in four areas: synagogue construction, Jewish education, interest in Bible study, and interest in Jewish theology and religious thought.[11]

Synagogue Construction

As mentioned at the beginning of this chapter, synagogues and temples were being built at a higher rate than ever before. Herberg noted that, "the expansion of the synagogue is, indeed, one of the most striking features of our time."[12]

In addition, Conservative Judaism, more so than the other movements, seemed to be thriving. According to Sklare, Conservative Judaism was faring even better than Christianity in the United States. Sklare wrote in 1972, regarding the previous two decades:

---

[9] Ibid., 189–190.

[10] Ibid., 190.

[11] Jonathan D. Sarna, *American Judaism: A History,* New Haven: Yale University Press, 2004, 279–281.

[12] Ibid., 190.

> Conservatism's prosperity is particularly note-worthy in its stark contrast to developments in Protestantism and Catholicism: Conservatism has experienced none of the reductions-in-force which have characterized the Christian community.[13]

Sklare also pointed out that in the sixties, Conservative Judaism far outstripped Reform and – more important for our story – Orthodoxy in terms of how Jews identified themselves. He cited statistics that showed this to be true for cities across the United States. For example, he quoted a survey taken in Boston in 1965 which showed that "44 percent of the Jews of that community thought of themselves as Conservative, some 27 percent thought of themselves as Reform, and 14 percent as Orthodox." Even in New York, where he presumed Orthodoxy to be stronger than anywhere else, he reported: "…it is apparent that even in the New York metropolitan area, more Jews would describe themselves as Conservative than as either Orthodox or Reform."[14] Regarding national figures, the American Jewish Population Survey of 1971, which gives figures for 1970, revealed that 40.5 percent of American Jews thought of themselves as Conservative. Only 11 percent said they saw themselves as Orthodox, one percentage point below those who said they felt "just Jewish."[15]

Yet, in spite of the fanfare, the promise of Jewish spiritual growth didn't materialize. Although more synagogues were being built, and identification with Conservative Judaism was very strong, one did not get a sense that there was an increased interest in what went on *inside* the synagogue. The same Marshall Sklare who cataloged the promise of Conservative Judaism and its sharp ascendancy in the 1960s wrote about synagogue attendance in that period:

---

[13] Marshall Sklare, *Conservative Judaism: An American Religious Movement.* New York: Schocken Books, 1972 (new, augmented edition), 253.

[14] Ibid., 254–255.

[15] National Jewish Population Study, "Jewish Identity: Facts for Planning," Council of Jewish Federations and Welfare Funds, New York: 1974, 1.

Many investigators have collected statistics on the question of attendance at worship. Their findings all point in the same direction: Jews attend religious services very infrequently.[16]

Jewish Education

Jewish day schools were beginning to emerge as an important force in Jewish education, and rabbis were being ordained by the various rabbinical seminaries, and placed in pulpits. Sarna pointed out, though, that, "as enrollment in Jewish schools *increased,* standards in Jewish education *decreased*" [Sarna's emphasis]. Any casual observer of Jewish education in America could see how few children were "turned on" by the "afternoon school" or "Talmud Torah," and how many were actually "turned off."

Bible Study, Jewish Theology, and Religious Thought

With regard to adult Jewish education, Sarna provided statistics that indicated a revival of interest in Bible study, Jewish theology, and religious thought:

> A great wave of interest in Bible study overspread the Jewish community, paralleling the Christian back-to-the-bible movement of the same period. In an effort to "reclaim the bible for the Jews" – a reference to the spate of novels and films that presented the Bible in a Christian framework that Jews found thoroughly alienating – numerous synagogues organized Bible classes, and Jewish home Bible study programs proliferated…. Between 1952 and 1954, sales of its [the Jewish Publication Society's] Bibles rose almost forty percent – perhaps in response to the number one bestseller of these years, the protestant *Revised Standard Version of the Bible.* In 1956, the bible or books about it constituted almost half of the *total* [emphasis his]

---

[16] Marshall Sklare, *America's Jews,* New York: Random House, 1971, 118.

number of books that the Jewish Publication Society distributed and sold....[17]

As interesting and encouraging as these statistics appear, they did not necessarily point to an invigoration of Jewish thought and Jewish activity. Sarna may have been correct about the revival of interest in Bible study, Jewish theology, and religious thought, but one wonders if these areas were being pursued primarily in institutions of higher Jewish education and rabbinical seminaries, and not trickling down to the average American Jew.

Regarding Sarna's statistics of sales of Bible-related books and the creation of Bible study groups in synagogues, it would be interesting if there were more detailed statistics available. What, for example, were the actual numbers of attendees at the Bible study groups in "numerous synagogues," and how many of the people who bought Bibles or Bible-related books actually read them? Furthermore, of those who did purchase and read Biblical materials, did that reading positively affect their Jewish life? Unfortunately, it seems that an in-depth analysis of those numbers does not exist, and so we are left wondering how relevant the statistics are.

The Vanishing American Jew

According to some, American Judaism was not only failing to invigorate Jewish thought and theology, but was fighting for its very survival. In just another generation, the Jews could vanish altogether from the American scene. This viewpoint found its most public expression not within the confines of the Jewish community itself, but in the wildly popular and non-Jewish American icon, *Look* magazine. In May, 1964, *Look* published an article containing dire predictions on the future of American Jewry under the audacious title, "The Vanishing American Jew."

Focusing mainly on the subject of intermarriage, the article projected that if the trend continued, Jewish identity in the United States would eventually become nonexistent. After stating that Jews no longer needed to

---

[17] Sarna, *American Judaism,* 280.

seek refuge in their Jewish identity and support Israel because anti-Semitism was on the wane, the article stated that, "Judaism, for all of its success, has failed to involve many Jews," with more than a third of all US Jews being unaffiliated with any synagogue. *Look* predicted that the next generation of Jewish college students "will conclude that Judaism has little or nothing to say to them."[18]

The article plagued both Jewish leaders and the rank and file. It was not so much that they believed its statistics and projections, but it was unpleasant and even frightening to be counted out by one's countrymen in a major national publication. Rabbis across the United States used the *Look* article as a springboard for sermons, classes, and discussion groups.[19] There is nothing like a doomsday scenario to provoke discussion as to why it is untrue.

The truth was that American Jews were not vanishing; the real danger to Jewish continuity lay in the fact that they were simply tired and apathetic. There was a sense of ennui and increasing apathy to the turbulence of this confusing decade. The sixties, primarily, were a period of change, and Judaism, especially Orthodox Judaism, was hardly changing.

The lack of spontaneous spirituality in the Jewish community lead them to believe that Judaism held little relevance to their lives. Just as some in the gentile population responded to the turbulent times by exploring alternative and sometimes cult-like movements, some Jews reacted to the confusion around them and joined these groups as well. "As many as six percent of the followers of Reverend Moon's Unification Church, twelve percent of the

---

[18] Thomas B. Morgan, "The Vanishing American Jew." *Look*, May 5, 1964, 45–46.

[19] Rabbi Riskin himself used the *Look* article as a jumping-off point for his thoughts on American Judaism. On February 26, 1967 (almost three years after the *Look* story was published!), he spoke to a group in Fairfield, Connecticut on the topic "Will the American Jew Vanish?" (Yeshiva University press release, January 30, 1967; from the Yeshiva University Archives).

Hare Krishna movement, and 2.5 percent of the Zen Buddhists were Jews, although Jews constitute[d] about 2.5 percent of the population."[20]

The main Jewish reaction, however, was to create of a new kind of spiritual congregation – the Havurah.

Havurah

The essence of the Havurah was the desire of some Jews

> to undertake willingly the observance of rituals in a like-minded community…[because of the] dissatisfaction with bourgeois society, the hunger for authentic community, the willingness to seek spirituality through rituals and communal living….[21]

Begun in 1960 by Rabbi Mordechai Kaplan, the founder of Reconstructionist Judaism, the Havurah was originally intended to serve as an informal group within a synagogue. Toward the end of the 1960s, however, Havurot (sing. Havurah) were being founded not as part of the synagogue, but independent of the synagogue as a reaction to its lack of spiritual content and intensity.

The main chronicle of the Havurot movement was *The Jewish Catalog*. Published in 1973, this work popularized alternative practices and rituals culled from various Havurot and explained them mostly to curious Jews who lacked knowledge and depth in the original traditional forms of Jewish observance.

---

[20] M. Herbert Danzger, *Returning to Tradition: The Contemporary Revival of Orthodox Judaism.* New Haven: Yale University Press, 1989, 77, relying on statistics from J. Gordon Melton and Robert L. Moore, *The Cult Experience,* New York: Pilgrim, 1982, 30.

[21] Oppenheimer, *Knocking on Heaven's Door,* 100.

By definition, Havurot were countercultural, and considering the fact that Orthodoxy was the most conservative of all the Jewish movements, it stood to reason that there were no Orthodox Havurot on the Jewish scene.[22]

Interestingly, the Havurah as a concept did not last, though some of its features were introduced into mainstream (mostly non-Orthodox) synagogues, such as greater group participation in the prayer service, the introduction of new prayers and group discussions of sacred text, as opposed to sermons given by the rabbi. Although popular and independent for a short time, Sarna writes:

> Havurot never replaced synagogues for the majority of American Jews. Most havurot, in time, either disappeared, evolved into larger and more formal prayer groups, or became attached to neighborhood synagogues.[23]

Modern Orthodoxy

So what was the state of Orthodox Judaism when twenty-three-year-old Rabbi Riskin prepared to assume his position at Lincoln Square Synagogue?

If one were to gauge the success of Orthodox Judaism by the aesthetics of its synagogues in Manhattan, one would be forgiven for concluding that Orthodoxy was thriving in the 1960s. A major complaint in America about Orthodox synagogues had always been that the synagogues were not aesthetically pleasing and that their services lacked decorum. By the 1960s, major Orthodox synagogues in Manhattan had overcome these problems. Their buildings were beautiful, even majestic, and well maintained, and their services were orderly. Well-to-do Orthodox Jews – of varying degrees of religious observance – had built their opulent synagogues and engaged their venerable rabbis.

---

[22] Nevertheless, it is interesting to note that many of the features of the Havurah – such as the spirituality of the prayer services, the focus on community and serious study with an emphasis on finding spirituality in the text had already been incorporated into the Lincoln Square service even before Havurot became popular.

[23] Sarna, *American Judaism*, 321.

Kehilath Jeshurun, the flagship Americanized Orthodox congregation on the East Side, was led by Rabbi Joseph Lookstein, who had succeeded magnificently in instituting a "reverential, orderly and ordered, contemplative and dignified, highly choreographed and ritualized service [which] appealed to Upper East Side Jews, bringing them into the sanctuary."[24]

However, beautiful as they were, Orthodox synagogues were failing to attract young people who grappled with deep questions about Judaism's laws and purpose; and religion – Orthodox Judaism in particular – seemed to be all about rules and restrictions.

Although such synagogues were open to anyone, their core membership was Orthodox – if not necessarily in personal observance, at least in preference of affiliation – and the concept of specifically reaching out to the non-observant and unaffiliated was non-existent at that time. That is not to say, of course, that rabbis did not change their congregants' lives and raise their level of observance; their synagogues, however, did not exist for this purpose.[25]

Another issue facing Modern Orthodoxy was that it had never really recovered from the blow it had received from the defection of Rabbi Mordechai Kaplan, founder of Reconstructionist Judaism, but formerly the

---

[24] Jenna Weissman Joselit, *New York's Jewish Jews: The Orthodox Community in the Interwar Years.* Bloomington, IN: Indiana University Press, 1990, 66.

[25] The Ramaz School, founded in 1937 and housed in and sponsored by Kehilath Jeshurun, was performing a unique kind of outreach to young students, not adults. It is fascinating to note that, according to Jeffery S. Gurock, in 1966 (shortly after Rabbi Riskin's arrival at LSS), only 165 of Ramaz's 683 students were from the local neighborhood; the vast majority came from the West Side and the Bronx (Gurock, *American Jewish Orthodoxy,* 442).

Regarding adult outreach, the situation is obviously very different now. Kehilath Jeshurun's mission statement on its website reads: "We also seek to bring those latter values [religious traditions, study of Torah, observance of Shabbat and *kashrut*] to our fellow Jews who, for one reason or another, are unaffiliated with religious institutions. We do this by providing an ambitious and extensive outreach program." See Chapter 12 for more about the influence of Lincoln Square's outreach success on other synagogues.

most prominent Orthodox rabbi in New York. Kaplan's first rabbinic position in 1920 was in Kehilath Jeshurun on the East Side. He helped found the Young Israel Movement which, in its time, was considered to be Orthodoxy's hope for survival in America. Kaplan also was the first rabbi of The Jewish Center[26] on the West Side, but resigned in 1922, proclaiming that Orthodoxy

> precludes all conscious development in thought and practice, and deprives Judaism of the power to survive in an environment that permits of free contact with non-Jewish civilizations.... [Judaism must] revitalize the entire system of ceremonial observances by adjusting them to the spiritual needs of our day.[27]

Kaplan's negative judgment that Orthodoxy had nothing to offer American Jews was extremely demoralizing, and Orthodoxy was left scrambling to prove itself. Even some forty years later, as Rabbi Riskin prepared to assume the pulpit at Lincoln Square Synagogue, Orthodoxy had yet to improve its image. Jews who searched for meaning in their lives looked to communes and Eastern spirituality, not to a congregation run according to the strictures of Jewish Law.

Was there a way to retain the laws, rituals, and tradition while still appealing to people's modern sensibilities? Could Orthodox Judaism somehow be reworked without throwing the baby out with the bathwater? The problem was that Judaism had previously undergone a radical reinterpretation which resulted in the birth of Reform Judaism.

The German reformers of the nineteenth century believed that by modernizing Judaism, they were preserving, not destroying, this ancient religion. Rabbi Samson Rafael Hirsch, the founder of modern German Orthodoxy, countered Reform Judaism by reinterpreting Orthodoxy so that

---

[26] The Jewish Center was – and still is – an Orthodox synagogue whose name echoed Mordechai Kaplan's concept of the synagogue as a "center."

[27] Jonathan D. Sarna, *American Judaism*, 244–245. Quotation taken from Mordecai M. Kaplan, "A Program for the Reconstruction of Judaism," *The Menorah Journal* 6 (1920): 181–196.

it would be relevant and meaningful to those who were tempted to accept the approaches of the reformers.

The chances of another Samson Rafael Hirsch emerging in the 1960s in America were remote. What was needed on the scene in the mid-1960s was not only a respected theoretician on Modern Orthodoxy but also an implementer, someone who could translate the *Torah im Derech Eretz* thinking[28] and the *Torah u-madda* philosophy[29] into contemporary language and get it "to the people."[30]

The 1960s was a time of searching for personal meaning. Jewish theology had been preaching for centuries that its concepts were eternal and the commandments that embodied these concepts – the *mitzvot* – were immutable. It was these commandments that were supposed to infuse life – in any decade, in any century – with meaning.

But was that working? Had it worked for decades in the United States outside the narrow confines of the already-Orthodox community? For

---

[28] Rabbi Hirsch in Germany had already developed the concept of *Torah im Derech Eretz* in which he formalized a philosophy that incorporated a practical response to modernity, stating that a Jew can observe the commandments of Judaism in a traditional way while still embracing modern society.

[29] Rabbi Joseph B. Soloveitchik, professor of Talmud at Yeshiva University and scion of a prominent Lithuanian rabbinical family, had expounded a system of thinking about Jewish Law which embraced secular philosophy. His way of thinking translated into Yeshiva University's *Torah u-madda* concept, the notion that Torah and general knowledge could be somehow combined and synthesized.

[30] Of course, Yeshiva University was steadily producing rabbis, most of whom held this philosophy. These rabbis were trying mightily to inspire and teach, and many of them did so successfully. What was missing, however, was a discernible trend, a perceivable movement, a communal sense, a palpable excitement, a perception of turnaround. I most emphatically do not wish to imply that individual rabbis were somehow not doing their job until Rabbi Riskin's arrival at Lincoln Square. But in the modern Orthodox world, there had yet to be a sense that this way of thinking could really work on a wider grass-roots level, that Jews could return to their tradition in significant numbers, and that Torah study for adults with no previous Jewish background could catch on as a trend.

Jewish Americans in general, was there any connection at all between the Torah's commandments and their identity as Americans?

In 1962, 394 Yeshiva University-ordained Orthodox rabbis were serving in pulpits in the United States.[31] Victor B. Geller, the Director of Placement for RIETS (The Rabbi Isaac Elchanan Theological Seminary – Yeshiva University's rabbinic studies division), paints a rather dismal picture of the American Orthodox synagogue and rabbi at that time:

> The synagogue was still Orthodox, but more out of habit than conviction. Mixed seating and other deviations from tradition were tolerated in more than a few communities. The membership was now largely American-born and educated. While the number of college educated congregants increased sharply, their Jewish knowledge was minimal.
>
> Their American-trained rabbi was a spokesman and a symbol, not a religious authority whose guidance was sought and followed. Nonetheless, he tried very hard to bring one *mitzvah* [commandment] at a time to one Jew at a time. His was a difficult and often lonely struggle.[32]

Geller's comments reveal that Orthodoxy in the 1960s was on shaky ground. Even Yeshiva University, which provided the American community with young Orthodox rabbis, could not effectively enforce Halacha (Jewish law) in many so-called Orthodox synagogues. Geller refers specifically to mixed seating of men and women during prayer, which is not permitted according to Jewish law. He also hints at other deviations, which probably included the cantor or prayer leader facing the congregation, as was popular in Conservative and Reform congregations, instead of the Holy Ark, as was the Orthodox practice, and perhaps the abbreviation or omission of certain traditional prayers as well.

---

[31] Victor B. Geller, *Orthodoxy Awakens: The Belkin Era and Yeshiva University*. Jerusalem, New York: Urim Publications, 2003, 240.

[32] Ibid., 227.

Deep down, it appeared that many Orthodox rabbis had lost hope for a real turnaround. Certainly, individuals in their congregations or on college campuses could become interested in Judaism, and occasionally even become Sabbath-observant and keep kosher. However, the idea of a movement of Jews demonstrating a deeper commitment to their religion just did not seem realistic in the 1960s.

So, what hope did twenty-three-year-old Rabbi Riskin have with a virtually non-observant Orthodox congregation, if it could even be called that? They were essentially a small group of Jews who were more interested in social get-togethers than prayer. This group of secular, well-educated Jews met in a converted professional apartment in the new and half-empty Lincoln Towers, located on the edge of Hell's Kitchen. What were the chances that this particular "congregation" in this particular location could ever grow and flourish?

❧ 2 ❧

THE PLACE

Urban Renewal

IT WAS THE MID-1950S, and the czar of redevelopment, Robert Moses, had a plan. As the head of the New York Slum Clearance Committee, it was Moses's intention to save the West Side of Manhattan from its crowded slums while completely revitalizing its atmosphere at the same time. In an extremely bold move, Moses proposed the Lincoln Square Urban Renewal Project in 1955.

This proposal included construction of a "cultural hub" of Lincoln Center (which incorporated the Metropolitan Opera, the New York Philharmonic, the New York State Theater, the Vivian Beaumont Repertory Theater, the Julliard School of Music, and the Library and Museum of the Performing Arts), the Fordham University Law School, the headquarters of the American Red Cross, an 800-car garage, a new public school, a fire station, a public band shell, and a 3800-unit middle-income housing development – Lincoln Towers. In order to accomplish all of this, Moses needed to displace 678 businesses and 5,268 households.[1]

In most cities with an urban-renewal initiative, the government cleared the slums from the area and provided the land and low-interest mortgages in exchange for promises that the projects would provide middle-income

---

[1] Alexander Garvin, *The American City: What Works, What Doesn't*. New York: McGraw Hill, 2002 (second edition).

housing.[2] In New York, Robert Moses insisted that the developers take responsibility for clearing the property and the relocation of tenants. Afraid of this responsibility, many developers would not get involved with Title I projects,[3] or if they did, they would drag their feet about the clearing of land and tenant relocation.

William Zeckendorf, one of America's master builders and real-estate developers, had no such qualms. By becoming the sponsor of several projects, including Lincoln Towers, he had managed to obtain substantial financial assistance from the government through the Federal Housing Act of 1949. Zeckendorf's company, Webb and Knapp, became the major redeveloper in New York.[4]

> Zeckendorf was a man who knew how to turn his dreams into reality. It was Zeckendorf who had transformed some East Side Manhattan slaughterhouses into the site on which the United Nations was built. It was Zeckendorf who pioneered urban redevelopment in New York, Washington, and Philadelphia, and who became the biggest exponent of the modern shopping mall. It was Zeckendorf who viewed the whole of America as a giant Monopoly board in which mammoth office towers such as the Chrysler Building were bought and sold almost at whim.[5]

Lincoln Towers

In the mid-1950s, William Zeckendorf had a new dream; one that would secure him a place in the history of New York City architecture. William Zeckendorf was going to build the most interesting and cutting-edge

---

[2] Michael Decourcy Hinds, "Lincoln Towers, Up for Sale, Called Likely Conversion," *New York Times,* December 2, 1984.

[3] Title I of the 1949 Housing Act authorized funds to localities to assist in slum clearance and urban redevelopment.

[4] William Zeckendorf, *The Autobiography of William Zeckendorf,* New York: Holt, Rinehart and Winston, 1970, 236–237.

[5] Cary Reich, *Financier: The Biography of André Meyer,* New York: William Morrow and Company, 130.

apartment project Manhattan had ever seen. Lincoln Towers, Zeckendorf's largest project to date, would be daring in so many ways. It would be situated on West End Avenue, between 66th and 69th Streets, on the edge of Hell's Kitchen, and would replace the slum tenements in an area whose future had seemed uncertain. It would not be another cookie-cutter project; each of the four huge towers would be unique, yet would relate to each other as a whole. The towers would attract middle-class tenants to the neighborhood – exactly the kind of tenants that Robert Moses and the Slum Clearance Commission were seeking.

Lincoln Towers was going to be Zeckendorf's crowning achievement, and to ensure its success, he hired the famous Chinese-born American architect I.M. Pei to be his architect. Pei's flair had previously been demonstrated on one of Zeckendorf's earlier apartment projects, Kips Bay on Manhattan's East Side. But Lincoln Towers, with its massive, flat frontage, was going to be far more exciting than Kips Bay. The model Pei came up with for Lincoln Towers was a cluster of structures of various sizes laid out in a way that would avoid the monolithic overtones that had plagued so many other apartment developments.[6]

Things, however, did not work out exactly according to plan. Zeckendorf's major investment banking firm for the project, Lazard Frères, knew that he had over-extended himself on the Kips Bay project and was determined that profits would not be eroded once more by overspending. Lazard therefore opposed Zeckendorf's plan to hire I.M. Pei as his architect, since his design ideas were just too expensive to carry out. Since Zeckendorf was also encountering financial difficulties with his other projects, he found it impossible to hold on to Pei. Ultimately, Pei left the project and a "cookie-cutter"-type architect was brought in to finish the job.

Even though it seemed that Zeckendorf had overcome his financial struggles by replacing Pei with the less talented but more affordable architect,

---

[6] Ibid., 137.

By early 1963... the noose was tightening.... Zeckendorf had no alternative but to liquidate his properties, one by one.[7]

Lazard Frères became increasingly anxious about its investment in Lincoln Towers. Even with I.M. Pei off the job, "costs were escalating alarmingly."[8] Lazard kept up the pressure on Zeckendorf, saying it wanted out of its investment. To relieve the mounting pressure, Zeckendorf lined up a new partner, the Aluminum Corporation of America – Alcoa. Ultimately, with Alcoa's help, Zeckendorf bought out Lazard's investment at a significantly inflated figure. In an effort to hold on – at least partly – to Lincoln Towers, Zeckendorf became briefly associated with some British investors.[9] However, his plans failed once again. In May, 1965, Webb & Knapp was forced to declare bankruptcy[10] and Alcoa took complete control over the project.

Little Boxes

Under the new architect's direction, Lincoln Towers was completed in 1964 and strongly resembled other projects in the New York area – huge, flat-faced buildings with identical facades, "exactly the kind of dull, anonymous towers that Zeckendorf was so ardently trying to avoid."[11] Folk singer Pete Seeger might have had Lincoln Towers in mind when he sang in 1963 at Carnegie Hall:

> Little boxes on the hillside,
> Little boxes made of ticky-tacky,
> Little boxes on the hillside, Little boxes all the same....[12]

---

[7] Reich, *Financier,* 142–143.

[8] Ibid., 139.

[9] Zeckendorf, *The Autobiography of William Zeckendorf,* 292–293.

[10] Reich, *Financier,* 144.

[11] Reich, *Financier,* 138.

[12] "Little Boxes," words and music by Malvina Reynolds, ©1962, Schroder Music Company.

Zeckendorf was not happy about the "little boxes." In one of the most poignant statements of his life, he summed up the Lincoln Towers saga by stating:

> Lincoln Towers was a big job, where we handled the relocations of tenants with dispatch and fairness, but I'm not proud of the final project; I am ashamed of it. For a relatively minor increase in costs, Lincoln Towers could have been one of the wonders of Manhattan, but this was not to be. When these towers are torn down, no one will mourn their passing....[13]

A Meeting of Minds – Alcoa and Lincoln Square Synagogue

Once the construction of Lincoln Towers had been completed in 1964, Alcoa was left with the formidable challenge of renting out all of their newly-acquired apartments. It was by no means clear that the enormous efforts of Robert Moses and William Zeckendorf to attract people to the Lincoln Square area would work, and in 1964, the year that Rabbi Riskin became rabbi of the Lincoln Square group, the jury was still out.

Rudy Treitel, an early Lincoln Square Synagogue member who moved into the area as a newlywed in 1964, recalled that most Jews at that time preferred to stay away from the West Side of Manhattan – which was dangerously close to Hell's Kitchen – and opted instead to live in the more desirable East Side.

He described how that situation turned around when Jack Verschleiser, another early Lincoln Square Synagogue member, made a suggestion that ultimately resulted in a mutually beneficial arrangement between Alcoa and the LSS group.

> As more and more people moved into the neighborhood, Alcoa was only able to rent the studio and one-bedroom [apartments]. The two- and three-bedrooms weren't going. So Jack went over to [Charles

---

[13] Zeckendorf, *The Autobiography of William Zeckendorf,* 238.

Urstadt,[14] a friend from law school who worked, first for Zeckendorf, and then for Alcoa Residences]... and said, "The only way that you're going to be able to sell [sic] the two- and three-bedroom [apartments] is if you make it interesting for families.... You'll have the Orthodox families who require larger apartments and, to that extent, you have to make this a community. Right now, it's not a community; why should people move here?"

Danny Mars, the founder of the early Lincoln Square Group, describes a subsequent meeting in which Alcoa offered the LSS group two professional apartments on the first floor of 150 West End Avenue, a Lincoln Towers building. Up until this point, the venue for the group's prayers and social get-togethers had been the meeting room in their apartment building on 303 West 66th Street. The LSS group recognized the potential of the apartments as a future synagogue and accepted Alcoa's proposal. They knocked down the walls that separated the two apartments and created a synagogue and an office. Alcoa also threw in an apartment in the same building directly above the synagogue for Lincoln Square Synagogue's new rabbi and his wife. According to Danny Mars, the rent was very low for these three apartments.

Alcoa's motivation for such a generous offer was straightforward: After riding the roller coaster with Zeckendorf, Alcoa Residences were in desperate need of assistance in renting out the apartments and making the project profitable. They were convinced that the LSS group, as it grew, could be of substantial assistance to them in filling up the vacant apartments in Lincoln Towers. Alcoa bought into an idea that was as yet undeveloped and embryonic: a religious Jewish presence would become part and parcel of the redevelopment of the Lincoln Square area, which was crucial not only to the future of the West Side, but also Manhattan.

But the best part was yet to come. Danny describes the last part of the meeting, in which the future home of Lincoln Square Synagogue was sealed:

---

[14] Mr. Urstadt has remained at the cutting edge of New York real estate. Since 1998, he has served as vice chairman of the Battery Park City Authority.

They showed us a big map of the whole area, and they said, "Look, we have this piece of land here at 200 Amsterdam Avenue [Lincoln Square Synagogue's ultimate home]." We said, "We'll pay $400,000 for this, but subordinated to a mortgage." We'd get a bank mortgage [backed by Alcoa], which is like unbelievable. Nobody would do that. We had no credentials!

In April, 1966, when plans for LSS's new building on Amsterdam Avenue were first announced, Vaughn R. Chase, president of Alcoa Residences, Inc., was amazingly open and direct about the relationship. "We are confident that our contribution to the Synagogue… helps create a better neighborhood for our residents. We're grateful for this kind of activity."

Danny Mars, in a similar announcement, responded in kind: "We're especially thankful to Alcoa Residences, Inc, for its assistance in getting the synagogue started. An agreement allowing us to buy the property at a cost substantially below the commercial value of the land made it economically possible for us to begin construction."[15]

God in a Secular City

Even though both Zeckendorf and Moses were Jewish, these two men would never have predicted that an Orthodox Jewish synagogue would prove to be a significant factor in their redevelopment of the Lincoln Square area. Surely young Rabbi Riskin, on the other hand, noticed, as he strolled the area in 1964, the fruits of Zeckendorf's and Moses's labor – the new emphasis on the notion of "a cultural hub." Philharmonic Hall had been housing concerts for two years and the New York State Theater had just opened. The symbol linking all of the Lincoln Center cultural institutions and the defining icon of Lincoln Center – the Lincoln Center Fountain –

---

[15] Fragment of document from Yeshiva University Archives, "Alcoa Aids Plans for Synagogue," dated April, 1966, apparently from a Yeshiva University press release. Appropriately, Vaughn Chase had been named the guest of honor at Lincoln Square Synagogue's First Annual Dinner in 1965.

had just begun to function. Rarely did cities have the preponderance of their major cultural facilities together in a unified location.

There was already a considerable Jewish population in the area, and it was common belief that many more Jewish families would move into the new Lincoln Towers.[16] The question, however, was, whether the new Lincoln Square Synagogue could provide a "Jewish cultural hub" amidst Lincoln Center's cultural offerings. In addition, could the Lincoln Square Synagogue congregants function as a Jewish community and be inspired to take an active interest in Bible, Talmud, and prayer in a city filled with alienating forces?[17]

In *The Secular City*, Harvey Cox notes that in the 1960s it had already become commonplace for the urban social system to be attacked for two presumably negative features: anonymity and mobility. Modern man, he says, is seen as a "faceless cipher," whose identity and selfhood have been lost in the depersonalizing urban setting. How can this lack of identity be reconciled with traditional religion, which talks of the human soul's individual uniqueness? The urban denizen is also always on the move, the city being seen as...

---

[16] Already in 1963, before Rabbi Riskin arrived on the scene, Danny Mars and his group were searching for Jews – and finding them – in the two buildings of Lincoln Towers which were already up. Danny recalls, "We sent out a two-part postcard and we went through a reverse telephone directory – everyone whose name sounded Jewish.... People... came out of the woodwork."

[17] It is interesting to note that throughout the years since the establishment of Lincoln Square Synagogue, "outsiders" will often mistakenly refer to the synagogue as "Lincoln Center Synagogue." Although it may simply be an understandable error, referring to the synagogue as "Center" has always demonstrated to me the very close conceptual association between the synagogue and the "cultural hub" that abuts it.

When Rabbi Riskin was asked to come up with a name for the synagogue in Hebrew, he chose "Merkaz ha-Torah," translated as "Center of Torah." Perhaps the use of the Hebrew for "Center" was meant to echo the notion of Lincoln Center's cultural hub, an association which is absent (except for the "Lincoln") in the synagogue's name in English.

a kind of staging area where people pause in their complex movements from one place to another. Not only do we migrate between cities in search of improvement, but we migrate within cities to find more convenient or congenial surroundings…. Everybody is going places, but what is happening to us as a people along the way?

High mobility does play havoc with traditional religion. It separates people from the holy places. It mixes them with neighbors whose gods have different names and who worship them in different ways.[18]

Cox's central thesis in his important book is that God can become a part of the "secular city" if the perceived problems of the modern urban setting can be turned into spiritual advantages.[19] For example, he shows that anonymity in an urban locale can lead to greater freedom of the spirit. In a small town one must be everyone's friend, while in a large city, one has the freedom, if one so wishes, to remain anonymous. Mobility, which has the great power to make human begins feel displaced and directionless, can also be, according to Cox, the key to social change. According to Cox, "Changes in one area of life – job or residence – will lead to other kinds of change." He adds, "Those who have been drawn into the tradition-demolishing orbit of urban life are never quite the same again."

Cox's challenge of bringing God to the "secular city" was, in a sense, also Rabbi Riskin's challenge. Just as Cox tried to redefine religion so that it could function in the modern urban setting, so would Rabbi Riskin need to reinterpret Jewish faith and Jewish practice in order to make them relevant to the urban Jews of the ever-changing New York City.

If Zeckendorf and Moses were not responding to the questions posed by *The Secular City,* they certainly were reacting to the phenomenon of urban alienation – and perhaps to the larger question of the alienation blanketing the country in the 1960s. Regarding the Lincoln Square area, both men

---

[18] Cox, *The Secular City,* 39, 49–50, 54.

[19] In the final analysis, of course, Cox is a Christian theologian, so some of his conclusions and suggestions simply do not fit into a Jewish theological context. However, his articulation of the urban situation vis-à-vis religion is extremely sharp, and some of his points do translate well into the Jewish framework.

wanted something which would soften the urban landscape; Zeckendorf wanted I.M. Pei's beehive-shaped, interesting-looking, variegated buildings, and Moses wanted – and got – a huge cultural center as the hub which radiated revitalization to the West Side. Perhaps Zeckendorf's shame over Lincoln Towers was not only an architectural response to the uniformity of the "little boxes," but also a reaction to his inability to transform his huge towers into a community.

Ironically, where Zeckendorf failed, Rabbi Riskin and Lincoln Square Synagogue succeeded. The dull, anonymous towers which Zeckendorf so despised became the very community base for Lincoln Square Synagogue. Although not all of the Lincoln Square Synagogue members lived in Lincoln Towers (such as the founding group from 303 West 66th Street), those towers represented the potential for the growth of the synagogue.

A synagogue in a large urban area – especially an Orthodox synagogue in which walking to services on Shabbat is encouraged – cannot effectively serve the entire city. It needs to draw upon potential congregants from the reasonably immediate geographical area. So, perhaps more so than any other religious or cultural institution, the new Lincoln Square Synagogue would be dependent upon community for its growth, flavor, and even its very existence.

In 1964, the West Side of Manhattan – particularly the Lincoln Square area – was in a crucial state of flux. Although the construction of Lincoln Towers had been completed and Lincoln Center was functioning, there was an underlying feeling of unrest in the area, largely due to the significant population transfer.[20] The Lincoln Square population needed to try to feel and act like a community. The softening of the urban landscape that Zeckendorf so desperately wanted to achieve through his original vision of Lincoln Towers was taking place in a converted professional apartment in

---

[20] Throughout his career, Robert Moses was severely criticized for displacing New York's low income citizens. While a discussion of this point is important, it is beyond the scope of this work. For our purposes, we must focus on the fact that Lincoln Towers was ushering in a whole new population, thus opening up the question of community.

one of the less-than-distinctive buildings which he constructed under duress. Robert Moses's brash attempt to perform radical surgery on the Lincoln Square area was being subtly altered through the teaching of the ancient words of the Jewish sages to an increasingly attentive audience. Finally, a young religious figure was speaking with charisma, authority, depth, and love about life, community, Jewish law, and urban alienation and its cures. After all its tumultuous experiences with the acquisitive Zeckendorf, Alcoa had made an investment in the quiet, wise and penetrating voice of Jewish tradition.

❧ 3 ❧

THE TEACHER

STEVEN RISKIN WAS BORN on May 28, 1940 to a non-observant Jewish family in the Bedford-Stuyvesant neighborhood of Brooklyn. His parents, Harry and Rose, attended synagogue just once a year on the High Holidays, and only then out of respect for Steven Riskin's maternal grandmother, Haya Bayla, or Baltcha, who was a deeply religious Jew from Poland.

When the time came for Steven to go to elementary school, his parents chose to send him to a yeshiva, a decision that was motivated not out of concern for his Jewish education but rather from a belief that he would receive a better general education there than in the neighborhood public schools.

When he was nine, Steven began attending a neighborhood *shtiebl* on Shabbat, an informal Orthodox prayer group which lacked almost all the trappings of a structured congregation. Eitz Chaim Anshe Lubien was his grandmother's *shul,* founded by her *landsleit* (countrymen) from Lubien. Rabbi Riskin recalls that "the congregants sat in the very rows in which they had sat in the synagogue in Lubien."

Even though he did not come from a religious background and had never set foot on European soil, Steven was deeply affected by the simplicity of the Yiddish-speaking worshippers who recited the prayer service by heart. The rabbi of the congregation, Aharon Dovid Zlatowitz, was so impressed by Steven's seriousness that he enlisted his help for the Yom Kippur service. Since the rabbi could not speak English, he asked the nine-year-old boy to prepare a brief sermon in English prior to the Yom Kippur appeal for donations so that the English speakers who attended the High Holiday services would be inspired to donate to the synagogue. Steven did so without hesitation, reporting even now that he felt no self-consciousness as a nine-year-old preaching to adults about giving charity.

As much as Steven was positively influenced by the prayer service at the *shtiebl*, nothing could compare to his grandmother's *davening* (prayer) at home. As a child, Steven spent every Friday night at his grandmother's house,[1] watching her "speak[ing] to God as to an old and trusted friend"[2] while she lit the Shabbat candles. Profoundly moved by her spirituality and sincerity, young Steven would mouth the words of the *Kabbalat Shabbat* (welcoming the Sabbath) service along with her. Unlike most women of her generation, Baltcha had been taught to study Talmud and was also deeply familiar with the Chumash, the written Torah. In addition to their time spent together in fervent prayer, she and young Steven studied together. Because Steven was an extremely bright child and loved to discuss ideas, he found the activity of studying Torah immensely enjoyable. He excelled in his studies at the yeshiva, but the time spent with his grandmother engaged in Torah study was qualitatively different. Their study sessions were filled with joy and love for the Torah, and Steven was inspired to live up to his grandmother's religious expectations of him. He recalls the following incident from his childhood:

---

[1] Steven's grandmother had fallen into a depression because her husband was in a coma after suffering a stroke. Aware that Steven was the light of his grandmother's life, his parents sent him to her house each Friday night in order to lift her out of her depression. Rabbi Riskin says it worked.

[2] Unless otherwise attributed, Rabbi Riskin's comments in this chapter and throughout the book, both those quoted directly and indirectly, were made in interviews with the author or appeared in one of three other places: 1) Rabbi Riskin's own unpublished notes; 2) the interview entitled "Ode to Grandma Batya" in *Pathways: Jews Who Return,* by Richard H. Greenberg, Northvale, New Jersey: Jason Aronson, Inc., 1997, 216–222; and 3) the Foreword to *Torah Lights: Genesis Confronts Life, Love and Family,* by Shlomo Riskin, Jerusalem: Ohr Torah Stone, 2005, 9–15.

One Shabbat morning, just as I left my house on the way to *shul*, two non-Jewish boys about my own age asked me if I wanted to go roller-skating with them in Tompkins Park. At first I refused, explaining that I didn't own roller skates. They said they had skates to lend me. I guess I must have wanted to be one of the guys after all. I'm sure that I already knew that roller-skating on Shabbat was wrong, but I don't remember being terribly conflicted. I had compartmentalized my "religious" life at my grandmother's house and in the yeshiva, and my more "secular" life at home, and I saw the roller-skating offer as a great opportunity to become "one of the guys." I went roller-skating together with them, and I felt very good. On the way home from Tompkins Park, with the roller skates slung over our shoulders, I spied my grandmother returning with some elderly women friends from... *shul*.... As I said, I didn't feel conflicted, and I did want to wish my grandmother a "*Gut Shabbos*." So there I was, the "yeshiva *bocher*" grandson, accompanied by two non-Jewish guys, roller skates over my shoulder, embracing my grandmother. She kissed me and wished me a "Good Shabbos," but for the first time, she looked at me with terrible disappointment.

I'd never, ever seen her look at me like that. She had always looked at me before with enormous pride. I even saw tears welling up in her eyes. That look in her eyes made me understand what I had done and I think that was the last time I was *mechallel shabbat,* the last time I ever knowingly desecrated the Sabbath. I think about that often, because, when I picture standing before God's heavenly throne, after 120 years, it is not His punishment that I fear. After all, God is Biblically described as "*Hashem, Hashem, Kel rachum v'chanun*" – the God of love, who loves you both before and after you sin, the God of infinite patience and forgiveness. I think of God with too much love to ever be fearful of Him or of His punishments; that, too, is one of the legacies I got from my grandmother. But I am desperately afraid that maybe He will be disappointed in me. I would never want God, or my grandmother, to ever again look at me in disappointment, with tears welling up in their eyes.

From an early age, Steven loved to study, and developed a respect for, and an attachment to, intellectual rigor and the search for a pure, unadulterated truth. However, as he matured and studied further, he understood that pure truth needed to be mitigated by love and compassion in the same way that God Himself mitigates pure justice with love when He judges humankind. This fusion within Steven's personality of what might be seen as conflicting forces – the search for pure truth on the one hand and the intense quality of empathy on the other – began with the model of his grandmother as his first real teacher of Torah and his mother's insight into unconditional love, and extended to his teaching and preaching throughout his career.[3]

Rabbi Riskin tells another touching story in which his non-observant mother was embarrassed because she was smoking a cigarette on Shabbat (which is not permitted by Halacha) when a religious friend of his came to call. After the friend left, his mother at first bemoaned the dissonance between her son's observance and her non-traditional feelings, but after a while, rethought the matter and declared, "God put us together on purpose so that you would learn to also love people who aren't religious."[4]

---

[3] Rabbi Riskin would frequently comment on the etymology of the word *rachum*, meaning compassionate, which the Torah frequently uses to describe God. Rabbi Riskin pointed out that *rachum* originates from the Hebrew word *rechem,* which means "womb." The implication is that God's compassion for human beings is compared to the deepest form of compassion known to humankind, the love of the mother for the child of her womb. Given the rabbi's seminal experiences of learning with his grandmother, and the pithy lesson of loving non-observant Jews from his mother, his attachment to the *rechem* image for God's compassion seems natural and meaningful. Rabbi Riskin recalls feeling deeply moved when he heard this imagery evoked on Yom Kippur night by Rabbi Yosef Shlomo Kahaneman, Rosh Yeshiva of the Ponevesz Yeshiva in Bene Berak, Israel, in 1960.

[4] The very fact that Rabbi Riskin tells this story, which shows great respect for his mother even as he describes her with a cigarette in her hand on Shabbat, is very significant. As the "Ba'al Teshuva (Newly Observant) Movement" grew in the late 1960s and 1970s, it was forced to deal with relationships between newly observant children and their non-observant parents. Across the spectrum of rabbis and yeshivot, varying advice was given regarding the tension between the Torah's commandment to honor parents and the sages' derivation from Torah verses that a

Steven's father, Harry Riskin, also instilled in his son the importance of reaching out to each and every individual regardless of his or her background. A salesman by profession, Harry opened up his heart to each person he encountered on a day-to-day basis, whether a family member or a stranger off the street. Rabbi Riskin puts it simply:

> He may not have taught me how to learn a page of *Gemara* (the Talmud, compendium of Jewish law and philosophy), but he did teach me lessons which are equally important: how to live, how to savor each moment of the joys of living, how to love, how to communicate with people, how to establish enduring commitments and relationships.

High School Years

Steven Riskin's high school years were spent at Yeshiva University's High School for Boys in Brooklyn, better known as Brooklyn Talmudical Academy, or BTA. Steven had been accepted to the vaunted Stuyvesant High School in Manhattan, but fate took a different turn. An administrator at BTA noticed him studying in the yeshiva library for hours on end during the summer, and was impressed by his intellectual curiosity and commitment to study. He offered Steven a full scholarship to BTA, the tuition for which his parents would never have been able to afford.

The school offered a reasonably high standard of Jewish studies, but many of the students did not take those studies seriously. In the first half of the twentieth century in the United States, it was common for American Jews to assert their American identity by de-emphasizing their Jewish

---

child may not violate a commandment even if a parent demands it ("Both of you [the child and the parent] are required to honor Me [says God]" – Talmud *Baba Metzia* 32a). Although the law is clear, the nature of the new relationship between newly religious children and their non-observant parents rested upon the nuances. From the cigarette story, it is clear where Rabbi Riskin stood on this advice-giving spectrum.

Eighth-grade graduation at Yeshiva of Brooklyn, 1952.
Steven Riskin, first row, second from left. Credit: Riskin family photo.

Rabbi Riskin's parents, Harry and Rose Riskin. Credit: Riskin family photo.

identity. The small percentage of American children who did attend Jewish schools were therefore not as serious about their Jewish studies as they were about their secular studies. Although there were some students who were interested in the impact of their Jewish studies on their religion – Steven Riskin among them – the atmosphere at BTA was hardly inspired.

The intellectualism which characterized Steven Riskin from a young age flourished, to a certain extent, during his high school years. From a social perspective, BTA was a very difficult setting for Steven; his academic ability and intense interest in study led him to be placed him in the highest level of Talmud lectures and classes, and as a result, he was separated from students of his own age group. He was only twelve years old as an entering freshman, yet he shared classes with seventeen- and eighteen-year-old students. The discomfort caused by the ridiculous social disparity, however, was ameliorated somewhat by Rabbi Harold Kanotopsky, his Talmud *rebbe,* who took him under his wing.

A master educator, Rabbi Kanotopsky understood Steven's predicament and attempted, albeit mostly unsuccessfully, to protect him from the pranks and practical jokes played on him by his older and far less serious classmates. More important, Rabbi Kanotopsky studied privately with Steven and responded to his many questions. Rabbi Riskin recalls that Rabbi Kanotopsky was his first real role model, and his brilliant tutelage provided Steven with the structure and freedom during his high school years to develop both on an intellectual and spiritual level. As his thinking matured, Steven became deeply disturbed by what he now refers to as "some of the fundamentalist views" of those around him. Even as a high-school student, Steven was less than satisfied with the conventional Orthodox explanations of major principles within Judaism. What was the Oral Law, exactly, and how had it come about? What, precisely, was the nature of God's revelation to the Jewish people and to the world?

In connection with these and similar questions, Steven Riskin began to read about Conservative Judaism, which claimed to have new insights and "modern" viewpoints on the very issues that troubled him so much. In fact, by his senior year in high school, he had become so interested in

Conservative Judaism that he seriously contemplated studying at the movement's flagship institution, the Jewish Theological Seminary (JTS) upon graduation.

After what he considered an enlightening discussion with the admissions officer at JTS about the subject matter he would be studying and the approach to that subject matter, Steven believed that at long last he would receive answers to his knotty theological questions. Following the interview, Steven wandered the corridors of the institution, deep in thought. He recalls an incident that took place during his walking tour of the halls of the Seminary. According to Rabbi Riskin, it was this incident that clinched his decision to abandon the idea of attending JTS.

> I saw a student walk up to a water fountain to take a drink of water. He turned on the water, leaned over – I was standing right there – and took a drink – without making a *bracha* [reciting a blessing over the water]. I knew right then and there that this was not the place for me. I said, "They're not serious. Nothing can come from people who don't make *brachot*."[5]

It is, of course, impossible to determine with certainty the relative weight of this incident in Steven Riskin's decision not to attend the Jewish Theological Seminary (which probably would have resulted in him becoming a Conservative rabbi). It is even difficult to surmise whether Rabbi Steven Riskin's immediate reaction to the incident actually happened in the way that

---

[5] I asked Rabbi Riskin to help me analyze his strong reaction to this incident and his rather harsh conclusion as to its meaning. I asked him, "What made it so obvious to you that nothing can come from people who don't make *brachot*?" He answered, "We're talking about *Avodat Hashem* [service of God]! We're talking about religion! I felt that this [religious commitment] is what... preserved us all the years and it's very important. That takes seriousness. That takes serious commitment. I was concerned about *Torah she be'al peh* [the Oral Law], Revelation and those kind of theological things. But clear to me was the importance of commitment.... The one thing that I did always sense was that you can't make changes unless you're committed to the fundamental system. Nobody can make changes in the system, tamper with the system, unless you're really seriously committed to the system."

he recalled or if this explication crept in later. However, the fact that Rabbi Riskin imputes such importance to the incident speaks volumes about the complexity of his theology.[6]

Now that the idea of attending JTS was out of his system, Steven Riskin faced a new and important decision as high school graduation from BTA fast approached. The Jewish Theological Seminary was not Steven's only institution of choice. An extremely bright and gifted student in secular studies, Steven had also applied to Harvard, and by the end of his senior year in high school, he received not only an acceptance to Harvard, but a full scholarship to that university. Naturally, his parents were elated. However, as much as the prospect of study at Harvard excited him, he was reluctant to turn his back on the world of the yeshiva. After all, that world had been so nurturing for him, and had introduced him to the "formal" world of Torah study, which became an extension of the Torah study so lovingly initiated for him by his grandmother.

Yeshiva University

Just prior to the deadline for his decision, BTA made arrangements for Steven to spend the holiday of Shavuot at Yeshiva University, where he would celebrate the holiday with the rabbis and students in the customary way of staying up all night to study Torah. When Rabbi Riskin now describes the experience, he emphasizes a moment of great emotion, when he (as a *Kohen*, descendant of the Priestly class) recited the Priestly Blessing[7] at the

---

[6] Rabbi Riskin is stating – and has stated for years through his teaching and personal halachic practice – that with all of the important theological pondering one must do, a Jew is responsible to observe all of the details of Halacha. His uniqueness emerges as a combination of components which was then, and sadly, continues to be, rare in the Jewish world – the scholar/teacher/rabbi who is punctilious about halachic observance, yet is willing to "push the envelope" when it comes to searching and striving for meaningful theological and philosophical answers about God and the universe.

[7] The Priestly Blessing is taken directly from Numbers 6:24–26: "May God bless you and keep you. May God illuminate His countenance for you and be gracious to

sunrise service together with the saintly Rabbi Yitzchak Lessin. This stately, white-bearded man, who served as the Yeshiva's *mashgiach ruchani* (spiritual adviser to students), evoked the holiness of the European yeshiva scene.

At that moment, two very disparate parts of Steven's life came together and moved him toward a decision.

> He [Rabbi Lessin] had a beautifully sweet voice and enhanced the words of the blessing with a long wordless melody that they used to sing in Slabodka. I felt it must have originated in the Holy Temple. I was moved to tears. I kept thinking of what my grandmother would want me to do.... Strangely enough, I also thought of my Communist grandfather, Grandpa Shmuel.[8] From the midst of the Priestly Benediction, I remembered Grandpa Shmuel teaching me to separate my fingers into the letter "*shin*," and telling me, "Remember, we are *Kohanim*, and that's Jewish royalty. Always be a proud Jew." All these thoughts went through my mind as my soul soared to the sound of the melody. Before *Birkat Kohanim* (the priestly Blessing) concluded, I had taken an oath to go to Yeshiva University.

---

you. May God lift His countenance to you and give you peace." Perhaps as a result of this experience, Rabbi Riskin never tired of explaining that the introductory prayer to this blessing emphasizes that the Priests are required to bless the people "with love."

[8] Rabbi Riskin's paternal grandfather was a communist and an atheist, and wrote a regular column for the Yiddish communist newspaper *Freiheit*. The rabbi recalls that as a young boy, he would join his Grandpa Shmuel in the *shvitz* on Myrtle Avenue in Brooklyn and they would discuss philosophy and politics. Rabbi Riskin says that discussing his grandfather's anti-religious views helped him clarify his thoughts about God, Judaism, and Torah. He also had great respect for his grandfather's idealism – his passionate belief that the world would be redeemed by communism. Ironically, it was Grandpa Shmuel who taught Steven – both of them descendents of the Jewish priestly class – how to form his hands and fingers for the Priestly Blessing. It puzzled Steven that this avowed atheist would even show any interest in such a purely religious act, until his grandfather gave the touching explanation about Jewish royalty, which entered Steven Riskin's mind and spirit on that Shavuot morning at Yeshiva.

This was a classic moment in Rabbi Riskin's life not only because the decision to attend YU assured his remaining within Orthodox Judaism or even because it was the next step on his career path to becoming an Orthodox rabbi. It was a significant moment because it contained a mixture of the cognitive and the affective that was to characterize Rabbi Riskin's personality and his teaching throughout his life. Although a committed intellectual, virtually every important moment in his life contained an element of high emotion and sentiment. Yeshiva University won out over Harvard not as a result of a comparison of their academic programs; on that Shavuot night Steven Riskin was moved to the core of his being by a spiritually uplifting experience at Yeshiva that he knew could not be replicated at Harvard. As a budding intellectual, he had harbored great expectations about what he could learn at Harvard; but as a Jewish soul burning with spirituality, he turned toward a source that would nurture that fire – the yeshiva.[9]

The Rav

Without question, Steven Riskin's major influence throughout his years at Yeshiva University was Rabbi Joseph B. Soloveitchik, of blessed memory, known in YU circles simply as "The Rav."[10] Steven immediately realized that being in Rabbi Soloveitchik's presence was being in the presence of

---

[9] Harry and Rose Riskin could not afford to pay Yeshiva University's tuition. The scholarship to Harvard, on the other hand, would have released them from any payment. A quirky but loving member of Steven Riskin's family came to the rescue. His great-aunt, Sadie Goldberg, marched with him into the office of Dr. Samuel Belkin, the President of YU, and demanded a full scholarship on the basis that her great-nephew was "a genius." To his credit, Dr. Belkin overlooked Mrs. Goldberg's unorthodox approach (the financial aid deadline had long since passed), tested Steven and granted him a full scholarship.

[10] Rabbi Soloveitchik (1903–1993), one of the most outstanding Talmudists of the twentieth century, was also one of its most creative Jewish thinkers. In North America, he was respected as the unchallenged leader of Modern Orthodoxy.

greatness, and the Rav's clarity and creativity of explication of the Talmud left young Riskin breathless.

> I began to realize that all that I was looking for – the spiritual, the intellectual, the humanistic – could all be found within the pages of the Talmud. I became a very devoted disciple of Rav Soloveitchik; my Yeshiva University experience was very much centered around the Rav, who became my religious and spiritual mentor.

Rabbi Riskin's statement is extremely important, and not only because he clearly states that Rabbi Soloveitchik became his *rebbe*;[11] almost every student of Rabbi Soloveitchik in those days was only too proud to consider the Rav as his *rebbe*. Unique to Rabbi Riskin's situation was that he absorbed and imbibed the Rav's teachings and philosophy so deeply that he was able to become not only the Rav's student, but also a teacher of the Rav's thinking before almost anyone else was doing it.[12]

In those years, Yeshiva University spoke proudly about the idea of "synthesis," which involved the melding of secular and religious studies in order to produce a new whole Jew, one who reflected on the values of Torah, yet still modeled the best of Western civilization's learning. There was always a great deal of discussion about how this synthesis should take place, which values should become paramount, and what would happen to those Western ideas that had no place within the Torah construct. However,

---

[11] For the serious adherent of Judaism, finding oneself a *rebbe* – a kind of "master Rabbi" – is crucial. While an individual may study with many rabbis, he needs to choose one rabbi who will be his constant spiritual guide. Because the purpose of Torah study is not for intellectual challenge alone, but also to apply what one has learned to one's life, much of the subject matter is open to subtle interpretation. The student therefore needs to find a *rebbe* whose interpretation and overall worldview make sense to the student in some holistic way.

[12] Chapter 6 discusses the details of Rabbi Riskin's presentation and "popularization" of Rabbi Soloveitchik's thought in the early days of Lincoln Square Synagogue, and how Rabbi Riskin caused the Rav's approach to pervade the synagogue.

synthesis – or Torah and *madda* (secular thought), as it was frequently called – was always seen as the goal.

Whether Steven Riskin had synthesis as his goal at that time is not clear. However, he approached both his secular and his religious studies at Yeshiva with such vigor and enthusiasm that he unconsciously became a model of such a synthesis. His secular majors were Classics (Greek and Latin) and English Literature, and his secular mentor was Professor of Classics Louis Feldman, who became a confidante of sorts as well.

Torah leadership seminar, December, 1962. "The Shofar Song."
Rabbi Riskin is second from right. Credit: Riskin family photo.

Torah Leadership Seminar

While Steven Riskin was pursuing his undergraduate degree at Yeshiva University, a revolutionary program was conceived by Dr. Abraham Stern, of blessed memory, Director of the Youth Bureau of Yeshiva University's Community Service Division. The program, which began in 1955, was called

Torah Leadership Seminar, and it brought several hundred Jewish high school youth from across the United States together, twice a year: during the winter vacation break in December, at a hotel, and during the final week of August, at a summer camp.

Dr. Stern, who came from the world of social work, was the first person in the Orthodox world to initiate the idea of bringing Jewish high school students with limited Jewish backgrounds together to study Judaism intensively, to experience Shabbat together, and to enjoy themselves.[13] As such, the Torah Leadership Seminar paved the way for all of the now-familiar modes of outreach (*kiruv*); principally the Shabbaton, or group Shabbat experience.[14]

Dr. Stern, reflecting on Seminar's success in 1967,[15] noted that those Jewish children who received a Hebrew School education – only to stop that

---

[13] It seems that the only other similar program in force at the time (from which Dr. Stern may have taken his inspiration) was the Brandeis-Bardin Institute in Simi Valley, California, founded in 1941, which ran a summer camp, and which was dedicated to helping young Jewish people discover and nurture their Jewish identities. Major differences between Torah Leadership Seminar and Brandeis-Bardin included the target age group (Brandeis-Bardin was for college and post-college people; Seminar was for high school students) and the fact that Seminar's agenda was the teaching of Orthodox Judaism in a happy, palatable way, while Brandeis-Bardin was Jewishly non-sectarian, and brought the message of both secular and religious expression of Jewish identity.

[14] Very little credit has been given to Dr. Stern (who died in 2006) for this monumental achievement. Although many organizations – some of them significantly to the religious right of Yeshiva University – began to adopt Seminar's approach after its success became apparent, I have never seen a single acknowledgement on their part regarding the origin of the idea. A comprehensive study on Torah Leadership Seminar's origin, development, and ripple effect is awaited.

[15] "Torah Leadership Seminar Bar Mitzvah Yearbook 1955–1967." Susan Schaalman, editor, prepared by The Youth Bureau, Community Service Division, Yeshiva University, with the participation of the Yolanda Benson Honor Society, 4–5.

education after bar or bat mitzvah – were often left with a very immature sense of what Judaism was all about. He identified that the high-school years were crucial in engaging the students' minds and hearts before all interest in their Jewish identity was lost. He was the first to ask the question:

> What then, is the prospect of reaching the large numbers of Jewish adolescents – the Day School and Talmud Torah graduates on the one hand, and the unaffiliated and the uninitiated on the other, who are drifting into a life of Jewish ignorance, and who will inevitably produce new and more shocking statistics of assimilation, intermarriage, and other serious, though perhaps less dramatic, manifestations of erosion from our ancestral faith?

Dr. Stern's answer was the Torah Leadership Seminar program.

> Torah Leadership Seminar was conceived to serve a dual purpose – 1) to educate, to enable teenagers to acquire knowledge, understanding and appreciation of their faith in a relaxed country setting conducive to learning, and 2) to simultaneously equip these young people with leadership skills – so that they could in turn impart new-found ideas and convictions to peers upon returning to local congregations and communities.[16]

Part of the secret of the success of Torah Leadership Seminar[17] was the quality of its teaching and the talent of its rabbinical staff. Already in 1961, two years before Rabbi Riskin's ordination, Dr. Abraham Stern recognized the young man's uncanny ability to connect with people and recruited him for the teaching staff. Steven Riskin threw himself completely into the

---

[16] "Torah Leadership Seminar Bar Mitzvah Yearbook 1955–1967," Susan Schaalman, editor, prepared by The Youth Bureau, Community Service Division, Yeshiva University, with the participation of the Yolanda Benson Honor Society, 4–5.

[17] Dr. Samuel Belkin, of blessed memory, president of Yeshiva University from 1943 until 1975, noted that, going into its thirteenth year, Seminar had already exposed "nearly 10,000 young people... to this imaginative and creative program" (TLS Bar Mitzvah Yearbook).

teaching at Seminar, and would often lend a lesson a kind of "revivalist" quality by gesticulating and even jumping in place to emphasize his teaching points.[18] With his ability to enthrall the participants, Riskin quickly became one of the most popular teachers at Seminar.

Even more powerful than Steven Riskin's effect upon the students at Torah Leadership Seminar was the effect of Seminar upon Riskin himself. As he beheld the transformative effect of the "Seminar approach" on its participants, Steven Riskin began to increasingly internalize the idea that, if educated with passion, people with no background could develop an insatiable desire to learn more, and moreover be moved to change thinking patterns and lifestyles.

Vicky Pollins

After his graduation from college in 1960, Steven Riskin spent the 1960–1961 academic year in Israel, where he studied intensely at the famous Ponevezh Yeshiva for the month of Elul, prior to the High Holidays. For the remainder of the year, he was enrolled in both the Hayim Greenberg Teachers' Institute and the Hebrew University. Through his studies and the experience of day-to-day living in Israel, he became very attached to the country, and considered remaining there. His parents in New York, however, were very resistant to that idea.

Toward the end of his Israel stay, he worked as a counselor for an Israel trip for American high school students sponsored by Yeshiva University. The trip also catered to a college-age group whose home base in Israel was Bar Ilan University. Although Steven Riskin was scheduled to speak to that

---

[18] The jumping and the gesticulations would later become part and parcel of Rabbi Riskin's teaching style at Lincoln Square Synagogue. Regular congregants became accustomed to their rabbi's individual style, and saw the physical motions as totally sincere and reflective of his bubbling excitement about what he was teaching. Outsiders or new members, on the other hand, sometimes felt a sense of puzzlement when they observed the rabbi in action. Could someone really be that excited about the Torah and Judaism? The answer was a resounding "yes."

group one morning at 8:00 a.m., he was unable to begin on time because one young woman, Victoria Pollins of Queens, was still fervently completing her prayers. Only Rabbi Riskin's own words can be allowed to express what he says was his emotion of the moment:

> I can honestly say that at that moment I truly fell in love with [Vicky] and decided that this is the person I wanted to marry.

Sixteen-year-old Vicky Pollins found herself praying in that synagogue at Bar Ilan at that moment in time as the result of a confluence of circumstances. From a non-observant, though pro-Jewish household, Vicky's parents believed in giving their daughter a "broadening" education, which included world travel. She had done the "European Tour" and wanted to explore Israel. In order to find the proper group for her, Vicky's mother went to a synagogue (for the first time in her life) in Queens and enquired about trips to Israel for young people. The executive director asked Mrs. Pollins, "Is your daughter observant?" Not realizing that the word "observant" is often a euphemism for "religiously observant," Vicky's mother replied proudly, testifying to Vicky's intelligence and alertness: "My daughter is very observant."

So began Vicky's odyssey in Judaism. The executive director of the Queens synagogue hooked her up with Yeshiva University's tour to Israel in the summer of 1960, which deeply inspired her and put her on the road to Jewish study and religious experience. Vicky was so enamored of Israel that she decided to join the YU Israel trip again the following summer, and thus found herself in the group that was addressed that July morning at Bar Ilan by Steven Riskin.

During their two-year courtship, which coincided with Steven's studies in the program for Rabbinical Ordination (Semicha) at Yeshiva University, the young rabbi-to-be was doubtful about a possible career at the pulpit. Aside from the fact that he genuinely felt that his personality was best suited to the profession of teaching, he had other doubts about becoming a pulpit rabbi. As a *Kohen*, a descendant of the priestly class, Rabbi Riskin was forbidden by Jewish law to come into contact with a corpse, making it impossible for him to officiate at a funeral in the presence of the deceased. Officiating at funerals was considered central to the list of a rabbi's congregational responsibilities. Even Jews who were distant from observance of most laws and customs usually turned to their rabbi when confronted with the death of a loved one.[19]

Rabbi Riskin's identity as a *Kohen* had triggered within him deep thoughts about the issues of *tumah* (ritual impurity) and *taharah* (ritual purity). He intuited the message – and later taught it boldly – that Judaism reinforces life and tries to move away from death. The newly-ordained Rabbi Riskin did not want to – and, as a *Kohen*, was unable to – serve a congregation in which he would need to focus on death.[20]

---

[19] Once Rabbi Riskin became rabbi of Lincoln Square Synagogue, the halachically acceptable solution occurred to him: he could conduct a funeral by reciting his eulogy before the remains of the deceased were brought into the building. Although this was an unprecedented way of conducting a funeral, the congregation soon adjusted to the change.

[20] Years later, at Lincoln Square Synagogue, Rabbi Riskin oversaw (but not directly, because of his *Kohen* status), the establishment of a *Chevra Kadisha* (literally, "The Holy Group"), a Burial Society. The *Chevra Kadisha* was founded at the initiative of Dr. Roy Stern, who, as well as being the rabbi's brother-in-law, was an active congregant. No other synagogues in the area had a *Chevra Kadisha*.

Although European Jewish communities traditionally relied on their own community members to perform the tasks related to the death of individuals, in America and in Manhattan of that day, the practice had become depersonalized, with funeral homes employing groups, usually made up of older people, to prepare the Jewish corpse for interment. The Lincoln Square *Chevra Kadisha* consisted of young volunteers, which reinforced the focus on life even in the realm of death.

The Lincoln Square *Chevra Kadisha,* like so many other areas of synagogue life at LSS, broke the contemporary mold. Dr. Stern recalls how the young volunteers, who were synagogue members, demonstrated compassion in their interactions with bereaved families. In addition to performing the required rituals in preparation for burial, they provided the bereaved with practical information on dealing with the funeral home, and they also offered sincere and heartfelt condolences on behalf of community members who had known the deceased.

Rabbi Riskin and Vicky, "A light moment." Credit: Riskin family photo.

Rabbi Morris Besdin speaking at LSS podium, 1975.
Rabbi Riskin and Vicky are seated behind him.

A Change in Direction

Immediately after Rabbi Riskin's ordination, beginning in the fall of 1963, he was engaged by Yeshiva University High School in Manhattan to teach a Talmud class. However, in June of that year, right after his wedding to Vicky, he was informed that the class had been cancelled due to lower-than-expected enrollment. Only several days later, before he had time to become concerned about having no job, he received a call from Rabbi Morris Besdin, of blessed memory, the Director of the newly formed Jewish Studies Program (renamed in 1965 the James Striar School of General Jewish Studies--JSS) of Yeshiva University. Rabbi Besdin offered Rabbi Riskin a teaching position in JSP.

The Jewish Studies Program was born as a result of Rabbi Besdin's uncanny perception of the contemporary "road map" of college-age Jewish young men in the United States at that time.[21] Although presumably no official survey was actually done, Rabbi Besdin was convinced that the religious mood of the 1960s had produced many Jewish high-school students who craved to know more about their Judaism. Rabbi Besdin, one of the first members of the educational staff of Torah Leadership Seminar, witnessed first-hand the thirst for Jewish knowledge among the unaffiliated high-school youth who joined Seminar.[22] But, historically and traditionally,

---

[21] Interestingly, Stern College for Women of Yeshiva University was founded two years before JSS began, and catered in good part to the female counterpart of the same target audience as JSS. Somehow, the notion of providing a basic level of Jewish studies for women seemed, at the time, less revolutionary that doing it for men. The difference, of course, was that JSS "impinged" on the prevalent notion of a "yeshiva," which was always seen as an academy for men studying Torah at a high level. There was no similar preconceived notion regarding such an institution for women.

[22] In an interview in 1967, Rabbi Besdin said that "JSS is the fulfillment of the desires stimulated by Seminar." He noted at that time that "approximately 20 percent of the applicants to JSS have been directed to the school by Seminar." (Gary Joseph Lavit, "A School is Born," in TLS Bar Mitzvah Yearbook, 27.)

like all other yeshivot, Yeshiva University only admitted students who had previously studied at yeshiva high schools, who knew the Hebrew language, and who had studied Bible and Talmud with the traditional commentaries. In addition to all of these requirements, the assumption – which was sometimes false – was that these young men, who had been (mostly) raised in observant Jewish homes, and who benefited from a yeshiva background, were themselves observant Jews.

In an interview, Daniel Besdin, son of the late Rabbi Morris Besdin (and a member of Lincoln Square Synagogue), explained that Rabbi Besdin's original inspiration – long before Torah Leadership Seminar – for creating the James Striar School came from his experience as a chaplain in the United States Army. Daniel recalled that Rabbi Besdin "was overwhelmed with the number of young [Jewish] soldiers he met who had no [Jewish] background…. [Rabbi Besdin] sensed that there was a tremendous hunger from these soldiers… [to] learn more about [their] religion…." Rabbi Besdin apparently saw no reason why young Jews entering college would be any less "hungry" than the Jewish soldiers whom he had met.

Rabbi Besdin was sufficiently excited about this to convince Dr. Samuel Belkin, president of Yeshiva University, to allow him to create and administer the new program. It was a revolutionary idea that was not met with complete excitement by many of the traditional European rabbis at Yeshiva University. However, it ultimately was approved, and proved to be one of the most successful academic – and spiritual – programs at Yeshiva University and in the Modern Orthodox world at that time. In a sense, the James Striar School could be seen as the first "Ba'al Teshuva Yeshiva" (yeshiva for the newly observant).[23]

---

[23] Beginning in 1967 in Israel, yeshivot for those who had no serious Jewish studies background began to emerge on the scene. (The first was The Diaspora Yeshiva on Mount Zion.) In parallel, the Sh'or Yoshuv Yeshiva, headed by Rabbi Shlomo Freifeld, opened that same year in Far Rockaway, New York. Even though the Jewish Studies Program predated these institutions by several years, JSP is seldom mentioned when Ba'al Teshuva Yeshivot are discussed, probably because it was part of an "establishment" institution, Yeshiva University.

JSS was a well-structured program that differed dramatically from the other religious studies programs at Yeshiva College, the undergraduate division of Yeshiva University.[24] The JSS program consisted of two classes per day, Monday through Thursday, from 9:00 am till 1:00 pm, in the following subjects: Hebrew Language, Bible, Mishnah, Talmud, and Jewish philosophy. The emphasis in JSS classes was placed on the study of the texts rather than general discussion.

JSS broke new ground by giving college students the possibility of studying the Jewish texts intensively without very much preparation prior to college. Jeffrey S. Gurock's research into JSS reveals that:

> The JSP's [JSS] core constituency during its inaugural era was... drawn from among those third-generation suburban Jewish families who had remained loyal to traditional ways and provided their boys with an adequate Jewish education through Hebrew schools.

> But it was the downgraded supplementary schools, those run by both Conservative and Orthodox congregations, that had failed their youngsters. It was as if the parents who had been sent to interwar Talmud Torahs and who later in their lives observed a modicum of traditions had had the JSP children who wanted as collegians to

---

[24] YU students had the choice of enrolling in one of three religious divisions. The central program of religious studies was RIETS (the Rabbi Isaac Elchanan Theological Seminary – later renamed YP, the Yeshiva Program), which involved thirty hours a week of intensive Talmud study. The other option was TI, the Teachers' Institute, which ostensibly existed in order to train teachers for Hebrew and Jewish studies, but which, in reality, was often selected by students for its greater concentration on the Hebrew language and Biblical studies and its lesser concentration on Talmud. Both of these religious divisions required an extensive background in both the Hebrew language and the methodology of the study of Rabbinic literature. In those times, one would only have such a strong background in Jewish studies if one had attended a Jewish day school prior to college. The third option was JSS.

become as Jewishly knowledgeable as their parents and decidedly more observant.[25]

In fact, the "supplementary schools" had failed virtually everyone, and those people made up almost the entire population of JSS. Dr. Abraham Stern had taken note of the irony: at the very time in life when young people started to develop their own thoughts, at the beginning of the formative years, it was exactly then that most after-school Jewish education stopped.[26]

---

[25] Jeffrey S. Gurock, *The Men and Women of Yeshiva: Higher Education, Orthodoxy, and American Judaism,* New York: Columbia University Press, 1988, 179–180. Since my book is not primarily about JSS, I rely on Professor Gurock's research regarding the makeup and motivations of the JSS students. However, Professor Gurock himself states (p. 258, n. 5), regarding incomplete archival material, that "when statements are made about the composition of the student body for any given time period, it is obvious that the findings are on the *observable* [emphasis his] members of the student body." Having attended JSS myself (1965–1968), my recollection (perhaps because it applied to me) is that, for many of us, our parents were not at all Jewishly knowledgeable and, in addition to wanting to be more observant than our parents, we wanted to know more than they did about Judaism.

[26] I heard Rabbi Riskin more than once, only partially facetiously, suggest changing the Bar-Bat Mitzvah (literally, one to whom commandments apply) to a *Bar-Onesh* (one to whom punishments apply) ceremony. The Torah technically prescribes punishments to those who violate its commandments (although, in practice, those punishments were rarely carried out). The minimum age of punishment is twenty. Rabbi Riskin was suggesting that, in that way, Hebrew schools would have to keep their students until age twenty rather than twelve or thirteen, which would allow them to instruct their students on a more mature level. Of course, though he was speaking in jest when he suggested a punishment ceremony, he was very serious about the ridiculousness of stopping Jewish education just when it could become meaningful to the young man or woman.

Approach and Methodology

At Rabbi Besdin's insistence, the teachers in JSS[27] taught Judaism through text; in Rabbi Besdin's language, the students were to study "It," not "About It." Until Rabbi Besdin's creation of JSS (and the later appearance of the "Ba'al Teshuva Yeshivot"[28]), this approach was not available to students without prior background. Many thought that it would be impossible for students of college age to begin to study primary texts, especially in the original Hebrew. Rabbi Besdin and JSS, however, proved the critics wrong, and Rabbi Riskin, having taught in JSS for a year before assuming the pulpit at Lincoln Square Synagogue, employed Rabbi Besdin's methods in the teaching of text.

In fact, in those early days of JSS, Rabbi Besdin became Rabbi Riskin's educational and rabbinical mentor. As much as Rabbi Riskin relied on his instinct with regard to teaching and connecting with his students and congregants, because Rabbi Riskin was not raised within the framework of a traditional synagogue, he had a certain deficit of knowledge and experience regarding "practical rabbinics." Although in some senses, this lack of knowledge helped Rabbi Riskin become creative and iconoclastic, in order to be an effective rabbi and educator he still needed to be able to grasp the nature of a tradition, approach, or custom before he could decide how far to go in reshaping it in his distinctive way. Rabbi Besdin provided this resource.

---

[27] The JSS story is one which should be told in full, if for no other reason than many of its graduates were inspired as a result of the program to study for the rabbinate, or, as informed Jews, to assume lay leadership positions in synagogues and Jewish schools in their later lives. Moreover, in my mind, JSS still stands as the model of a rigorous yet spiritually-laden approach to teaching uninitiated Jews. Finally, Rabbi Besdin was such an interesting and complex personality that a study of his life and career would be very edifying.

[28] Even in many of the "Ba'al Teshuva Yeshivot" (Yeshivot for those with no previous background in the study of primary Jewish texts), study is accompanied (and sometimes replaced) by a heavy dose of religious hortatory lectures (*mussar*), an approach which Rabbi Besdin felt was inappropriate for JSS.

But their relationship went far deeper than that. For all of the years he taught in JSS, Rabbi Riskin and Rabbi Besdin would share a two-hour lunch break together every Monday through Thursday during the academic year. What was the content of these lengthy and frequent conversations? Rabbi Riskin explains:

> Rabbi Besdin loved to monologue – and I became his most ardent listener. He was for me a *rebbe*, a mentor, a personal counselor, and a second father: every skill I acquired in educational methodology, every new initiative I established in the formative years of my rabbinate, every attitude I developed in my approach to Judaism and to life – were shaped by this generous, genuine, wise, incisive, and consummately normal *talmid hacham,* who was both modest and decisive, inspiring and down to earth, completely devoid of any modicum of self-importance or hypocrisy.[29]

⇛ ⇜

It was clear to Rabbi Riskin's students that in addition to his deep knowledge of Talmud, Halacha, and Jewish History, he was also a very deeply educated person in many areas of Western thought. The message was clear: An individual highly educated in secular studies could also lead a seriously informed religious lifestyle. It was this "synthesized" Rabbi Riskin who appeared to the early participants in Torah Leadership Seminar, at the James Striar School and, ultimately, at Lincoln Square Synagogue.

---

[29] Shlomo Riskin, "Rabbi Moshe Besdin – The Master Educator," *The Commentator* (Yeshiva College Student Newspaper), February 15, 2005. In a recent conversation with me, Rabbi Riskin added that these lunches were so important to him that on the days he taught in JSS, he never scheduled any meeting at Lincoln Square Synagogue until 3:00 p.m. so that he could keep his regular appointment with Rabbi Besdin.

Although Rabbi Riskin was a self-confident person who was aware of his strengths, he was sensitive to the fact that he lacked certain perspectives that come as a result of growing up in the Orthodox Jewish world. The rabbi therefore felt that he could learn a great deal from Rabbi Besdin.

PART TWO

THE MESSAGE

"It was a happening."

– Lenore Brown

Lenore and Jack Brown were members of Lincoln Square Synagogue in the early days, and I asked Lenore to summarize in her own words the "Lincoln Square experience." She thought back to the 1960s and answered, "A happening."

A happening is the culmination of events and experiences at a certain moment in time, which, when combined with historic forces and a specific ideological message, results in a dramatic artistic phenomenon. The Woodstock Music and Art Festival of 1969, which was perhaps the seminal countercultural event of the sixties, was described by Life Magazine as being:

> less of a pop festival than a total experience, a phenomenon, a happening, high adventure… and, in a small way, a struggle for survival.[1]

---

[1] "The Phenomenal Woodstock Happening," *Life* Magazine, September 15, 1969.

Life Magazine understood that the Woodstock experience was greater than the sum of its parts. What took place there was more than just an earthbound concert. Certainly drugs, music, and free love were rampant, but it was more than that. Interpreted through the lens of the 1960s, the event metamorphosed into a "happening," a piece of art that shed a bright and revealing light on the power of counterculture in America. Woodstock was a "happening" which brought American countercultural forces into the open, and consequently drew into those forces thousands of people previously unaffected by any countercultural trends.

In the same vein, what took place in Lincoln Square Synagogue under Rabbi Riskin was a "happening." It offered many of the features of a traditional synagogue: religious services, study classes, Shabbat and holiday celebrations, bar and bat mitzvahs, weddings, funerals. Yet, embedded within all of these activities was a message that transformed individual activities into a collective work of art. Lincoln Square Synagogue, under Rabbi Riskin's guidance, was a "happening" that revealed to a new generation the power of Jewish community, prayer, Torah study, Shabbat and holiday observance, and joy before God – all within the context of Halacha, Jewish Law.

Life Magazine pinpointed the Woodstock Festival as representing, "in a small way, a struggle for survival." Orthodox synagogues in the mid-1960s were engaged in a similar battle. They were failing miserably at revealing the inherent spirituality of Judaism and the compelling force of Jewish law to young non-observant Jewish professionals. Therefore, the survival of Modern Orthodoxy on any serious scale was in jeopardy.

Without the Lincoln Square "happening," the future of Modern Orthodoxy in America might have been severely threatened. This is true not just because of the numerous young (and some older) professionals at Lincoln Square who became religiously observant. It is true because Lincoln Square Synagogue was responsible for an unprecedented breakthrough in Modern Orthodox thinking. For the first time, outreach to the uncommitted became part and parcel of an Orthodox synagogue's planning, thinking, and programming.[2]

Woodstock's message had to do with the effect and role of music in the American counterculture. Lincoln Square Synagogue's message had to do with the relevance of Judaism's most traditional approach (Orthodoxy) to an American society that was undergoing massive

---

[2] See Chapter 12 for a full discussion of this turnaround.

upheaval in the 1960s. The "happening" of Lincoln Square Synagogue was not only complex but was also difficult to pin down since no unified, all-inclusive, detailed message was ever proclaimed. It was embedded deeply in a series of programs, events, sermons, classes, and discussions, and the hidden quality of this complex message often makes clear identification of it in all of its parts elusive and intricate.

But pin down the message we must, because it lies at the heart of the success and distinctiveness of Lincoln Square Synagogue. We will identify the message by analyzing the activities and events of the synagogue, Rabbi Riskin's communication of their purpose and meaning, and the reaction of those who participated.

4

LINCOLN SQUARE SYNAGOGUE'S NEW RABBI

IT WAS 1964, and Danny Mars's Conservative group was looking for a rabbi to lead their High Holiday services. Sydney Trompeter, one of the members of the group, suggested that they be in touch with Yeshiva University's Community Service Division for help. Dr. Samuel Belkin, the university president, informed of their inquiry, was aware of this group's potential to affiliate with the Orthodox movement if led by a dynamic rabbi.

He decided to send them the newly ordained, and highly intelligent and charismatic Rabbi Steven Riskin.

Rabbi Riskin first met with the Lincoln Square founding group in May 1964. Actually, the meeting itself was based on a misunderstanding. In order to "repay" YU for the full scholarship it had awarded him, the newly ordained Rabbi Riskin had agreed to aid Yeshiva's Community Service Division (CSD) in its community activities. Each weekend, Rabbi Riskin found himself in a different community, talking about the values and ideals of Orthodox Judaism as part of YU's plan to establish beachhead synagogues in these cities. After Dr. Belkin received the call from Danny Mars regarding a rabbi for the High Holidays, CSD asked Rabbi Riskin to meet with the group. Rabbi Riskin recalls that he made it clear to CSD that he was not interested in being a candidate for their rabbinical position, even just for the holidays. He would meet with the Lincoln Square group, but only for the purpose of speaking to them, as he was doing in various other communities, about the beliefs, practices, and relevance of Orthodox Judaism. The meeting took place in Sidney Trompeter's home, and Rabbi

Riskin recalls that at the end of a long evening, the Lincoln Square group offered him a position for which he did not know he was a candidate.

Rabbi Riskin was in a quandary. He was, of course, flattered and pleased to have been offered a position that seemed to have such potential. Staunchly committed to Halacha, however, he believed that a synagogue must have a *mechitza* (*mechitzot* pl.), a physical partition separating the sexes during prayer. Among the many symptoms of the disaffection with Orthodox Judaism in the 1960s was the open enmity displayed toward any physical partition in the synagogue. Many synagogues with *mechitzot* were being forced by their Boards of Directors to remove these partitions and create mixed-seating synagogues.

Lincoln Square Synagogue was founded as a Conservative congregation. Giving expression to the American penchant to avoid extremes, the Lincoln Square group opted for the movement in the middle. Reform Judaism seemed too far removed from tradition, while Orthodox Judaism was far too strict and old-fashioned; a movement more appropriate for European immigrants than modern Americans. Conservative Judaism was the choice of so many often simply because it stood between Orthodoxy and Reform. Sociologist Marshall Sklare, attempting to explain how Conservative Jews defined themselves in the 1960s, wrote:

> While some individuals define themselves as Conservative because of their alienation from Orthodox practice, others define themselves from the opposite direction – they point out that they are Conservative because they are not *Reform* [emphasis his]. Here again, theology is not involved.[1]

In an irony born of ignorance and a lack of serious Jewish education, the vast majority of Jews in America – including our Lincoln Square founders – made their choice of "stream" not on the basis of the theology of the movements or even their platforms on social action or Zionism, but rather on the most superficial of externals – the mixing of genders in synagogue seating. Although this requirement was just one of numerous strictures

---

[1] Sklare, *Conservative Judaism*, 206.

which characterized Orthodox-style prayer, the *mechitza* discussion seemed to take on a life of its own. No longer seen as just a vehicle of Jewish law for the purpose of adding the element of sexual modesty during the prayer experience, the *mechitza* symbolized to its opponents an antiquated need to de-emphasize sexuality and a dramatic departure from a mode of religious worship – mixed pews – which had become the norm in Christian America. Herman Wouk wrote at the time about the *mechitza* issue:

> A variety of arguments has been thrown up on both sides of this touchy point, which – I am almost ashamed to record this, but it is the truth – is the biggest religious issue today in American Jewry. What we have is a head-on clash of American manners and Hebrew forms.[2]

Yeshiva University's CSD, responsible for the placement of its graduate rabbis, was doing everything it could to deal with this new reality: They were obviously anxious to maintain the standards of Halacha in the synagogues that YU served, but pragmatically, they still needed to find positions for its rabbis.

Victor B. Geller, then Director of Rabbinic Placement for CSD, writes candidly that "the single issue that dominated CSD's efforts to increase its placement program was synagogue seating." He states:

> There was no more vexing problem facing the Orthodox community during the third quarter of the twentieth century…. When a congregation did agree to consider a RIETS [acronym for the Rabbi Isaac Elchanan Theological Seminary, Yeshiva University's rabbinic studies division] *musmach* [ordained rabbi], the issue of mixed seating was invariably the biggest obstacle.[3]

---

[2] Herman Wouk, *This Is My God: The Jewish Way of Life,* New York: Pocket Books, 1974 (revised edition), 119.

[3] Geller, *Orthodoxy Awakens,* 217, 220. The centrality of the *mechitza* debate in those years cannot be overemphasized. Nearly ten years after Rabbi Riskin began his tenure at Lincoln Square Synagogue, I assumed the pulpit of a small synagogue in upstate New York, with a *mechitza.* At least once a week I would be confronted by a

There seemed to be very little chance that the Conservative Lincoln Square group would agree to erect a *mechitza*. After all, Yeshiva University had made it perfectly clear that they were willing to provide them with a rabbi even without one.

Before Rabbi Riskin could make a definitive decision about accepting Lincoln Square's offer, he needed to seek advice from a halachic source that he respected. He decided to consult his revered teacher, Rabbi Joseph B. Soloveitchik. Surprisingly, Rabbi Soloveitchik discouraged Rabbi Riskin from taking the position, noting that the chances were slim that the group could be talked into a *mechitza*. Rabbi Soloveitchik also expressed concerns for Rabbi Riskin's career were he to accept his first position in a mixed-seating synagogue.[4] Rabbi Riskin told the Lincoln Square group that he could not accept their offer.

The very next day, Rabbi Riskin was summoned by Dr. Belkin, president of Yeshiva University, demanding to know why he turned down the position. As soon as the rabbi explained that he had consulted his Rosh Yeshiva (literally, the "Head of the Yeshiva," traditionally the rabbi who has the final word in Jewish legal decisions for his yeshiva), Rabbi Soloveitchik, Rabbi Riskin realized that he had stepped into the thicket of Yeshiva University politics. Rabbi Riskin recalls that Dr. Belkin, in a tone bordering

---

congregant or a board member (including my own president!) about the possibility of removing the *mechitza*. Of course, I was frustrated with being "stuck" on that topic; I wanted to discuss other aspects of Judaism with my congregation. The members who came to my classes and listened to my sermons began to realize that there was a great deal more to talk about in Judaism beside the *mechitza*. Those who did not engage in study remained obsessed by the topic, probably because it was so visible and symbolic.

[4] Rabbi Soloveitchik's hesitation seems strange considering his tacit permission for YU rabbis to start their careers in mixed-seating synagogues in order to change them. Perhaps Rabbi Soloveitchik – along with almost everyone else at the time – was certain in his mind that this West Side group of Jews was so removed from the idea of a *mechitza* that it seemed ludicrous even to try. Another possible explanation is that Rabbi Soloveitchik may have seen such potential in Rabbi Riskin that he did not want to see his career compromised in any way.

on sarcasm, told him, "Tomorrow your Rosh Yeshiva will tell you to accept the position."[5]

Rabbi Soloveitchik did indeed recant. He told Rabbi Riskin that Dr. Belkin, who happened to live on the West Side, was in a much better position than he to determine the potential of the neighborhood. Perhaps, opined Rabbi Soloveitchik, the congregation was new and impressionable enough to change its attitude towards the *mechitza*. He retracted his previous advice and now advised Rabbi Riskin to accept the position.

Rabbi Riskin, now in a true state of confusion, decided – interestingly and somewhat surprisingly – to consult the Lubavitcher Rebbe.[6] The Rebbe, who granted Rabbi Riskin a middle-of-the-night meeting, firmly encouraged him to follow Rabbi Soloveitchik's (latter) advice. He expressed the idea that

---

[5] Dr. Belkin was the president of Yeshiva University. Rabbi Soloveitchik, clearly the spiritual and intellectual center of the Rabbi Isaac Elchanan Theological Seminary (RIETS), YU's rabbinical division, held neither an administrative position nor an official administrative title. This arrangement allowed Dr. Belkin to dictate policy. Rabbi Soloveitchik, who preferred to see himself as a "teacher," generally avoided becoming involved in administrative matters. It was in the "grey" areas, such as this one, in which Rabbi Riskin was asking his teacher's advice on a matter in which the YU administration was already involved, that the roles of teacher and decision-maker overlapped. Hence, there was a tension between Rabbi Soloveitchik's advice and Dr. Belkin's wish.

Victor B. Geller writes in *Orthodoxy Awakens* (265): "Some critics have charged that his [Rabbi Soloveitchik's] self-defined role as a teacher was also a convenient shield which he used to protect himself from the unpleasantness of stormy confrontations with Belkin."

[6] Rabbi Riskin recalls that this spur-of-the-moment decision to speak to the Rebbe (Rabbi Menachem Mendel Schneerson), whom he had never met, was born of his conceiving of the Rebbe as the leader of his generation, in the sense that he took responsibility for Jews worldwide. This is interesting, because although Rabbi Schneerson, who had become the Rebbe of Lubavitch in 1950, had begun in 1964 to train emissaries to reach out worldwide to unaffiliated Jews, the Rebbe and the movement were still not that well known outside of Lubavitch circles. There is a certain prescience in Rabbi Riskin's having chosen the very founder of the Jewish outreach concept as his adviser for this fateful decision.

the ends justified the means and that it was more important that Rabbi Riskin accept the position at Lincoln Square, even in the absence of a *mechitza,* than miss the opportunity to encourage his congregants to become religiously observant.

Now buoyed by two high-level rabbinical *heterim,* or halachic dispensations, Rabbi Riskin returned to Rabbi Soloveitchik to tell him that he was going to accept the position. At that meeting, Rabbi Soloveitchik presented three stipulations to Rabbi Riskin's acceptance of the position: Rabbi Riskin could not actually reside in the community until there was a *mechitza,* but must stay in someone's home or a hotel for Shabbat and Holidays; the rabbi could not accept any remuneration for his services until a *mechitza* was present;[7] and finally, without a *mechitza,* Rabbi Riskin could not pray together with the congregation, but rather should pray earlier by himself and be present in the services only to explain the prayers and teach the congregation.

Rabbi Soloveitchik also stipulated that Rabbi Riskin should inform the congregation that he would not pray with them without a *mechitza* because if they assumed that the rabbi would pray without one, they would be much less apt to make the change.[8]

The Lincoln Square leadership[9] agreed to these stipulations, and in September 1964, Rabbi Riskin led his first Lincoln Square Rosh Hashana

---

[7] Since Rabbi Riskin could not accept a salary from the synagogue until it had a *mechitza,* Yeshiva University provided him with a stipend of $2,000 upon accepting the position.

[8] Rabbi Soloveitchik's final stipulation proved to be extremely difficult, considering what would be the natural reaction to a congregation to a rabbi who did not pray alongside them. It is unclear how effectively this was communicated to the congregation. Danny Mars recalls feeling surprised and somewhat hurt when he found out at a later time that Rabbi Riskin had not actually been praying with the group.

[9] When I asked Danny Mars, the founder of Lincoln Square Synagogue, how many people were on the Board at the synagogue, his answer was: "Don't ask. We invented something that everybody could be on the board. We had two boards. We

service at the Esplanade Hotel. The Rosh Hashana service was a resounding success, with a turnout of over two hundred people, and the Lincoln Square group was extremely satisfied with Rabbi Riskin's explanations and teachings at the Rosh Hashana service and with the regular Shabbat services that began that December.

However, it was more than the exquisitely clear explications of Jewish law and philosophy, expertly delivered, that began to excite the congregation. Rabbi Riskin was a warm, compassionate, and engaging human being, and bonded almost immediately with the worshippers. From the very beginning, he made a point of getting to know each and every congregant and cared deeply for their welfare. Consciously or not, through his approachability and friendly demeanor, Rabbi Riskin revealed his soul to his congregation.

Joel Wachs was a twenty-two-year-old college graduate when he first attended Lincoln Square Synagogue. It is obvious from the language that Joel used that even though it had been over forty years since he first met Rabbi Riskin, he was still deeply affected by that encounter:

> I had never seen a rabbi smile before.... I didn't know that a rabbi was allowed to smile. Now you get some idea of the impact Lincoln Square Synagogue had on me.... It was the enthusiasm, the vitality, and the caring. [I had been attending the Bible class for] just three or four weeks.... Then [Rabbi Riskin] hit me with, "Why don't you come to my house for Shabbat?" Well, I was just blown away.... [My previous rabbi] wouldn't have known me if I fell over him on Broadway....

Inspired by the rabbi's deep involvement in the synagogue and obvious caring for its members, the leadership realized that in order for matters to proceed, the rabbi needed to move physically into the Lincoln Square community. Rabbi Riskin had made it clear, though, to the Lincoln Square community that not only would he not reside in the community until a

---

had a board of directors and a board of governors, so anybody could be on the board."

mechitza was erected, he also would not pray with them on Friday night. He did, however, suggest a creative compromise which would satisfy his Conservative congregants.

Every Friday evening, in addition to the regular service welcoming the Sabbath, which was held at around sunset-time, Rabbi Riskin led a kind of pseudo-service later in the evening for the staunchly Conservative members. This Oneg Shabbat (literally, "enjoyment of the Sabbath," usually referring to a get-together held on Shabbat, with refreshments) service did not contain the "official" halachic elements of a regular service – Cantor Sherwood Goffin, who also led the regular services, would sing sections selected from the traditional services, followed by a talk given by Rabbi Riskin or a guest speaker on popular Jewish contemporary topics. Because of its status as a pseudo-service, Rabbi Riskin felt comfortable with the idea of mixed seating within such a setting. Moreover, the anti-*mechitza* congregants were also content that they were sitting together for what *they* considered the main service of the week.

Rabbi Riskin demonstrated not only inventiveness but tremendous courage in suggesting the late-Friday night service, which could have created an association in people's minds between the synagogue and the Conservative approach to Judaism.

When Rabbi Riskin first started leading the Shabbat services at LSS in December of 1964, he and his wife Vicky stayed at a hotel every Shabbat. They lived in Washington Heights during the week, since it was close to YU, where he taught at JSS. After the birth of their first child, Batya, on January 27, 1966, they stayed at his in-laws' apartment for Shabbat, which was on the 29th floor of a building on Central Park South, some distance from Lincoln Towers, where the new synagogue was located. Since Shabbat prohibitions prevented him from using the elevator, he walked these 29 floors six times each Shabbat – up after the early service, down before and up after the late "service," down and back up Shabbat morning, and down on the way to *Mincha* (the Afternoon Service) on Shabbat afternoon.

Leon "Muk" Eisenmann, an Orthodox Jew from Switzerland and a long-time member of Lincoln Square, recalls Rabbi Riskin's honesty about the absence of a *mechitza*, and his confidence that one would be installed. Muk tells of his first visit to a Friday evening service in the very early days:

> There was this young guy [Rabbi Riskin] jumping up and down, full of enthusiasm. He thanked me [for coming] and I said, "Well, what do you do Shabbat morning?" He said, "Well, Shabbat morning is not yet for you; we have no *mechitza.*" [Friday night was not a problem because there were no women in attendance.] The Rabbi said, "I guarantee you within three months, we will have a *mechitza.*"

Fully aware that Rabbi Riskin was not going to budge on the issue of the *mechitza*, Danny Mars suggested that the Board vote on the *mechitza* question at their upcoming meeting in March of 1965. In a move that would characterize Rabbi Riskin's leadership of the synagogue for many years to come, he clearly drew the lines of authority. "The Board," he told Danny, "does not vote on a Halachic issue. Let the Board vote on the renewal of my contract for whatever period it wishes. But with me comes the *mechitza.*"

In March 1965, as the Board prepared to vote on the extension of the rabbi's contract, and therefore the *mechitza*, an incident occurred that could easily have spelled the end of Lincoln Square Synagogue as an Orthodox institution and Rabbi Riskin's tenure as spiritual leader.

Rabbi Riskin was interviewed by Trude Weiss-Rosmarin, editor of *The Jewish Spectator*, a well-written and widely read newspaper published in New York. Weiss-Rosmarin had attended a Shabbat service at Lincoln Square, with the awareness that there was no *mechitza*. Rabbi Riskin, somewhat naïvely, gave her an open and lengthy interview, emphasizing the potential of the synagogue and his hopes and aspirations for its development. Following the interview, Weiss-Rosmarin published an article entitled "Orthodoxy à la Lincoln Square."

Although her article did reflect the synagogue's potential, Weiss-Rosmarin tried to demonstrate what she saw as the hypocrisy of Orthodox Yeshiva University serving a mixed-seating synagogue with one of its rabbis.[10] She also strongly implied that YU was more interested in extending its influence in Manhattan than remaining firm on Halachic issues:

> Rabbi Riskin told me that Rabbi Belkin and himself are certainly not happy with this situation, but "unless we make concessions, the synagogue will drift and affiliate with a non-Orthodox group."[11]

Of course, this article – and especially the reaction to it in the right-wing Orthodox *Jewish Observer* – did not sit well with Dr. Belkin at Yeshiva University. Only several days after the publication of the article, Dr. Belkin showed Rabbi Riskin a sheaf of letters from YU supporters expressing their anger with YU's inconsistent stand on the *mechitza*, withdrawing their support or threatening to do so. Rabbi Riskin recalls that at that juncture, he envisaged the end, if not of Lincoln Square Synagogue, then certainly of Yeshiva University's association with it.

Astonishingly, however, Dr. Belkin demonstrated commitment to Lincoln Square's cause even in the face of adversity. He not only told Rabbi Riskin that YU would continue its support of the project, but he handed Rabbi Riskin a personal check for membership dues in Lincoln Square. "Rabbi Riskin," he said, "if anyone dares to criticize you about the synagogue, just tell him that Dr. Belkin, the president of Yeshiva University, is a member of your synagogue." Rabbi Riskin notes that Dr. Belkin continued to send in his membership dues to the synagogue until his death in 1976.

What was Dr. Belkin's motivation for this act of solidarity? Did it indicate a semi-official weakening of Yeshiva University's – and, therefore, Modern Orthodoxy's – halachic position on the *mechitza* issue? Was it, as Trude Weiss-Rosmarin believed, a shamelessly opportunistic move on the part of YU, who wanted to see their influence greatly enhanced in mid-

---

[10] When Weiss-Rosmarin wrote the article, she was unaware that there was any possibility of a *mechitza* being installed in Lincoln Square, since Rabbi Riskin had thought it improper to confide in her information about the proposed Board vote.
[11] Trude Weiss-Rosmarin, "Orthodoxy à la Lincoln Square," Letter from New York, *Jewish Chronicle,* December 18, 1964, 8.

Manhattan by this new, dynamic rabbi? Could it have been a lack of judgment on Dr. Belkin's part, not understanding how destructive the "feeding frenzy" of those forces to the Orthodox right of YU could be, armed with "proof" that YU does not uphold Halacha? Or, perhaps more simply, yet more profoundly, did Dr. Belkin feel a sense of great confidence in the young rabbi who stood before him, who showed determination in finding new and creative ways to uphold Orthodox standards while still reaching out to non-observant Jews?

Whatever the reason, Rabbi Riskin's spirits were bolstered by the show of solidarity from Dr. Belkin. The Board met and voted to renew Rabbi Riskin's contract, and in March 1965, Lincoln Square Synagogue erected its first *mechitza*.

Left to right: Dr. Samuel Belkin, President of Yeshiva University; unidentified, Danny Mars, founding president of LSS; Rabbi Riskin. Credit: LSS archives.

✑ 5 ✑

THE SYNAGOGUE AS A SPIRITUAL CENTER

THE BATTLE FOR THE MOST VISIBLE SYMBOL of Orthodox Judaism, the *mechitza*, had been won. One might assume that now that Lincoln Square Synagogue was more visibly in the Orthodox camp, the synagogue might have conformed to the prevailing trend in every stream of Judaism, which was to strongly affirm its loyalty to the tenets – and even the "politics" – of its particular stream. In a front page article in the Lincoln Square Synagogue Bulletin of November, 1965, however, only a few months after the installation of LSS's first *mechitza*, Rabbi Riskin seemed to lead the synagogue in a different direction. In an article, significantly entitled "Our Credo," Rabbi Riskin stated:

> The Lincoln Square Synagogue is sponsored by Yeshiva University and is dedicated to the proposition that traditional Judaism can be meaningful for modern man. *We are attempting to disregard the usual labels of Orthodox, Conservative and Reform* [emphasis mine] in order to create a Spiritual Center [capitalization his] rooted in the eternal truths of Jewish Law which is at the same time able to reach the most marginally-affiliated Jew.

The "credo" goes on to describe both the mixed-seated (using those words) late Friday night Oneg Shabbat, and the "traditional practice" (separate seating) Shabbat morning service. Before concluding with a statement about the importance of adult education, the credo delivers the expectation that:

... with love and understanding we hope to minister to the religious needs of every son and daughter of Israel within the harmonious scope of our Synagogue in order to educate a searching generation to ultimately accept and appreciate the abiding values of our tradition.[1]

In "Our Credo," we have a truly amazing document both in its openness and in its presentation of an entirely fresh approach. While the message of the credo could on some level be interpreted as a clever public relations exercise, it is still remarkable that the word "Orthodox" only appears once in the credo, and only then in order to inform the reader that the synagogue is "attempting to disregard" the label.

To understand how remarkable this bold statement was, it is beneficial to examine the specific wording of the credo.

- "sponsored by Yeshiva University" – The opening phrase declaring a Yeshiva University sponsorship lent a certain level of status and even an academic tone to the Credo, and to the synagogue itself. In light of the fact that Yeshiva University was an Orthodox institution, Rabbi Riskin's eschewing of labels, including that of "Orthodox," was especially courageous.

- "We are attempting to disregard the usual labels of Orthodox, Conservative and Reform" – This statement is extraordinary. Virtually all of Jewish life in America in 1965 fell into one of these three categories. By renouncing these labels, Rabbi Riskin's statement flies in the face of the very organizational underpinning of US Jewry. In fact, the credo contains a strong hint of what would later be called transdenominationalism, which was espoused by Jewish groups beginning in the late 1960s, primarily by Rabbi Zalman Schachter-Shalomi's Jewish Renewal organization.

Transdenominationalism was born out of the sense that the use of labels in reference to the various movements within Judaism not only made it impossible to define each movement's theological and spiritual standpoint

---

[1] Although the article is unsigned, Rabbi Riskin confirms that he is the author.

but, more importantly, was suppressing their impact by placing too much emphasis on the political and institutional aspects of American Judaism. The Havurah movement of the late 1960s and 1970s, which sought to deemphasize denominationalism, acted as the inspiration for the publication of the various volumes of *The Jewish Catalog*, which became the "Bible" of transdenominationalism and Jewish Renewal.

Although Rabbi Riskin's seeming foray into the transdenominational realm in "Our Credo" would seem to hint at a spiritual alliance with these groups, Rabbi Riskin did not attach himself to them in any way, and in fact sought to distance himself from them, citing their lack of full commitment to Halacha.[2] It seems that Rabbi Riskin was trying to define a different type of transdenominational or post-denominational Judaism – a Judaism unburdened by labels but governed by Jewish law.

- "a Spiritual Center rooted in the eternal truths of Jewish Law" – The use of the term "Spiritual Center," especially with its capital letters, is important to our understanding of Rabbi Riskin's attempt to disregard labels. The word "center" had been used since the beginning of the twentieth century in connection with Jewish institutions. The original idea of the "Jewish center" was that it

---

[2] Rabbi Riskin tells a humorous story of paying a Shabbat visit to Havurat Shalom, America's first Havurah, in 1968. He felt that since the Havurah movement was so cutting-edge and was attracting disaffected Jews, he should see Havurat Shalom, under the leadership of Rabbi Art Green, up-close. Rabbi Riskin describes sitting on the lawn, davvening with the group on Shabbat morning, when someone sitting next to him interrupted him by offering him something. It took a few minutes for him to understand what was being offered to him, but when Rabbi Riskin realized that it was marijuana "in order to improve his *kavvanah*," he knew that the Havurah experience was not for him. Aside from the amusing picture this story evokes, it also illustrates the distance between the rabidly iconoclastic, anti-establishment culture of the Havurah on one hand and the mildly countercultural atmosphere created by Rabbi Riskin at Lincoln Square Synagogue on the other. Yet this clear differentiation is somewhat clouded by the startling "attempt to disregard" the movement labels as stated in "Our Credo."

would be a service agency, offering a variety of activities and social benefits to its mainly Jewish constituents, a communal gathering place…, a[n]… institution fostering Jewish culture and Jewish education… *an alternative* to the synagogue.[3]

Rabbi Mordecai Kaplan amended this idea and envisioned a "synagogue center," which would be neither a synagogue, nor a Jewish school, nor a social club like the YMHA, but rather a combination of all three. The term synagogue-center came to be defined as:

> Any combination of a synagogue and a center. This applies to a Jewish institution that combines the "religious" activities of the synagogue (worship, study, and public assembly) with the social services of the community center recreation, special interest clubs and informal education.[4]

Rabbi Riskin was familiar with the prevalent trend of synagogue "centers" being used for activities that had little to do with Judaism, and was determined to add a new meaning to the word "center."[5] He therefore

---

[3] David Kaufman, *Shul with a Pool: The "Synagogue-Center" in American Jewish History.* Hanover, NH: University Press of New England, 1999, 3.

[4] Ibid., 4.

[5] Rabbi Riskin recalls in the early days of Lincoln Square walking into the newly-formed Men's Club, which gathered in the synagogue one night during the week to play cards. With uncharacteristic anger, he picked up the gambling money which was on the table, threw it in the garbage can, and said, "This is a synagogue. It is not a gambling joint. And there won't be any gambling as long as I am the Rabbi here." He remembers the president of the Men's Club turning red in the face and saying, "You've just lost your Men's Club." "So be it," Rabbi Riskin answered. "Good-bye and good riddance!"

The rabbi had a clear vision of the ultimate purpose of the synagogue, and card-playing was not part of it. Hence the importance of his choice of phrase "Spiritual Center" in place of the "synagogue center" or "Jewish center," which was in general use, but which implied – to Rabbi Riskin – openness to activities unrelated to spirituality or inimical to it. In this light, it is easy to see how the rabbi chose

coined a new term, a "Spiritual Center," which encompassed Kaplan's notion of a gathering place but at the same time elevated the *purpose* of the gathering to one of spirituality.[6] He was determined to use the concept of a "center," but he wanted to co-opt it for the purpose of encouraging his congregation to strive towards *spiritual* rather than communal goals.

- *...rooted in the eternal truths of Jewish Law which is at the same time able to reach the most marginally-affiliated Jew* – This idea was not espoused – at least, officially – by *any* Orthodox synagogue at the time, and would actually have been seen by the Orthodox establishment as being paradoxical in the extreme: How could a synagogue that is "rooted in the eternal truths of Jewish Law" manage "at the same time... to reach the most marginally-affiliated Jew"?

In the 1960s, a huge chasm existed between the adherents of a strict interpretation of Jewish law on the one hand and the needs of the marginally-affiliated Jews on the other. This gap can in part be attributed to a lack of knowledge among marginally-affiliated Jews of the requirements of the Law and the lack of a willingness on the part of any particular Orthodox synagogue to welcome marginally-affiliated Jews. The most obvious and crucial obstacle, though, was the fact that marginally-affiliated Jews were not able to bridge the gap because they were not aware that such a chasm existed.

- "With love and understanding" – As strange as this may sound today, these words would not have been associated with Orthodox Judaism in 1965. Orthodox Judaism at that time was so concerned and preoccupied with maintaining standards of Jewish Law and practice that the human elements of "love and understanding" often did not enter into the equation. By using these words, Rabbi Riskin

---

"Mercaz Torah" – "Torah Center" – for the Hebrew name of Lincoln Square Synagogue.

[6] It should be noted that spirituality was a word that only came into general use in the realm of religion in the 1990s.

was well on the way to creating a new Orthodox Judaism, which was strong enough to uphold standards of Jewish law without losing sight of the importance of compassion and love. The significance of these words and their active implementation served to empower Rabbi Riskin's congregants and students. The message was clear – people who fell short of Orthodox standards in their personal life could still feel "loved and understood," and as a result of such positivity, were often impelled to strengthen their belief and level of observance.

- "A searching generation" – Rabbi Riskin was sensitive to the opportunities that the 1960s presented to him and his congregation. By presenting to Lincoln Square Synagogue an awareness of the societal search for meaning in life and for new modes of self-expression, he created an open atmosphere in which exploration and Jewish spiritual growth were given a framework.

- "Accept and appreciate" – It is hard not to hear in these words the echo of the Israelites' statement at Mount Sinai: "*na'aseh ve-nishma* – We will do [the commandments, and then] we will understand [them]." The commentaries point out the strange, seemingly illogical order of these verbs. Why would the people commit to performing the commandments before trying to understand them? The classical answer, frequently emphasized by Rabbi Riskin, is that, very often, a prerequisite for understanding is action. Part of the understanding of the concept of the commandment is found in its actual observance. Rabbi Riskin expanded upon this concept by encouraging observance of commandments – like prayer, group Torah study, and Shabbat observance – to be accompanied or immediately followed by a class on the topic. Of course, this approach was not enforced coercively; one could feel comfortable in the synagogue without observing anything. But the message of *na'aseh ve-nishma* – accepting and appreciating – was made clear. Rabbis at that time were constantly demanding observance; what made Rabbi Riskin different was that he was adhering much more closely to the Biblical model – observance and understanding.

૭ ઉ

What was the message that Rabbi Riskin was communicating to the congregation regarding Orthodox Judaism, and where did the congregation stand on the spectrum of Jewish movements in America? There was no doubt that Rabbi Riskin clearly saw himself as Orthodox and the synagogue as Orthodox. Having said that, Rabbi Riskin did not see himself working through the movement (or movements, because the Orthodox establishment in America was not – and never has been – monolithic) of Orthodox Judaism in order to bring Jews closer to Judaism.

It is possible that he merely felt restricted by lines drawn by those who spoke for Orthodox Judaism, but perhaps it had more to do with Rabbi Riskin's frequent declaration that he "never grew up in a shul." He was therefore unaware of the old tried-and-true litanies about what was accepted synagogue practice and what was not, since he had not been exposed to synagogue life as a child. So, in a sense, Rabbi Riskin created his own set of standards and practices. These practices were, of course, based on Halacha, as he understood it, and as it was interpreted to him by others, primarily by Rabbi Soloveitchik.

This approach can clearly be seen in his attitude towards the *mechitza*. Rabbi Riskin made it abundantly clear that the synagogue had to erect one, not because this was Orthodox practice or because it was required for membership in any particular Orthodox synagogue group, but rather because it was Jewish law. Though this may seem like a trifling difference, it was distinct enough to give the synagogue a more independent flavor than a typical Orthodox synagogue. It did not mean that activities that deviated from Orthodox practice were necessarily taking place, but when some things were done slightly differently, the reason was always explained, and it always made sense.[7]

Once again, Rabbi Riskin trusted and acted on his instincts, based on a deep inner awareness of what he wanted to achieve, and did not allow himself to become caught up in what other Orthodox synagogues were doing at the time. Such confidence was a real achievement in the realm of religion in general and Orthodox Judaism in particular, which is by nature conservative. Rabbi Riskin maintains to this day that it was his ability to act on his instinct which allowed him to be so successful at Lincoln Square.[8]

---

[7] In the traditional prayer book (*siddur*), the Friday night Shabbat service includes a section called *Ba-meh madlikin*, taken from the *Mishnah* (the essential book of Oral Law, written down around 200 CE), which describes the laws of lighting Shabbat candles. This section is sandwiched between two portions of the Friday night service and is supposed to enable the worshipper to study a portion of the Oral Law relating to Shabbat. In general practice, because the laws are quite technical, the section is recited quite quickly, and, unless that part of the *Mishnah* is familiar to an individual, he or she will probably not focus on the meaning of the passages and will therefore not benefit from a "study experience," which apparently was the original intention behind its inclusion.

From the start of Rabbi Riskin's career at LSS, Rabbi Riskin replaced *Ba-meh madlikin* with the actual study of a single, brief *Mishnah* from the tractate of *Shabbat*, with a full explanation and even response to questions. No other Orthodox synagogue that I know did this, and I even remember some criticism from outside the synagogue, complaining that Rabbi Riskin had "amended" the traditional service. The rabbi's intent was simple and clear: the purpose of *Ba-meh madlikin* was to engage in Torah study about Shabbat. That wasn't happening; let's make it happen. This idea would probably not have occurred to an Orthodox rabbi who had grown up in an Orthodox synagogue. If it did, he would probably be too "nervous" about making a change which differed from what he always had done. What is also important here is Rabbi Riskin's rarely failing instinct about what could be changed and what could not. Reform Judaism, and Conservative Judaism to an extent, had made changes which could not be supported by Halacha; on the other hand, Rabbi Riskin had a deep sense of which could and which could not.

[8] Rabbi Riskin recalls that in the early 1970s, Rabbi Yitzchok Hutner, head of the famed Chaim Berlin Yeshiva in Brooklyn, asked to see him. Apparently Rabbi

The Sound of the Shofar

During the first six years of Rabbi Riskin's career, the synagogue membership at Lincoln Square Synagogue rose dramatically, and as a result, the converted apartment at 150 West End Avenue was no longer big enough to accommodate the growing number of congregants. In 1971, the congregation moved from the apartment facility in Lincoln Towers to the beautiful and architecturally bold new building at 200 Amsterdam Avenue.

With each year that passed, Rabbi Riskin earned the deep and growing respect and admiration of his congregants, but by the time they moved to their new location on Amsterdam Avenue, he was still essentially a local figure. A local observer would be able to discern that the scope of activities and learning programs that were available in Lincoln Square Synagogue made this synagogue radically different from other Orthodox synagogues, but the "world" was essentially unaware of the revolution. On October 4, 1971, all of that changed. On that date, *Time* Magazine published an article about Rabbi Riskin and Lincoln Square Synagogue in its Religion section entitled, "The Sound of the Shofar." After interviewing Rabbi Riskin, the author likened the young rabbi to a shofar, describing him as "calling nonreligious Manhattan Jews to God."

The *Time* article is interesting and important for many reasons. First, it put Rabbi Riskin and Lincoln Square Synagogue "on the map."[9] *Time* didn't

---

Hutner had heard of Rabbi Riskin's success in bringing many alienated Jews back to Judaism. Rabbi Hutner wanted to know from Rabbi Riskin his methodology – the secret of his success. Rabbi Riskin told him that in all honesty, he really operated by "instinct." He says that Rabbi Hutner replied that all great educational and religious accomplishments are brought about by "instinct." It is unclear whether this is "good news" or "bad news," because it may beg the question of whether successes by outstanding individuals can be replicated.

[9] Several weeks after the *Time* article came out, we were sitting in the Lincoln Square *sukka* on the Shabbat of *Sukkot* listening to Rabbi Riskin teach his regular Shabbat afternoon Talmud class. In the middle of the class, a woman whom none of us knew stepped into the *sukka* and stood near the entrance. Rabbi Riskin paused, looked toward her, and said, in his always-friendly way, "Please, sit down, join us in

frequently feature rabbis, and would certainly have no reason to write about a typical rabbi of a typical synagogue. And so, if there was any question about whether Rabbi Riskin was special, or whether Lincoln Square was distinctive, the article in *Time* provided a definitive "yes."

But more importantly, Rabbi Riskin defined a new Orthodox Judaism for all of America to see, which may be what the *Time* editors sensed when they decided to publish the article. Although many sentences in the article are devoted to depicting Rabbi Riskin as a *wunderkind*, the author made several salient points about Rabbi Riskin's theology and his world view, the very points that could ultimately become defining qualities of a new Orthodox Judaism. At the time, the general public lacked the perspective which would allow them to recognize that a new Jewish identity was being defined, yet several of the concepts which Rabbi Riskin described in this article were revolutionary. The following are the main ideas expressed by Rabbi Riskin which appeared in the article. After each quote is a brief note on how Rabbi Riskin's view differed from the prevailing norm or impression:

- "The most important function of the synagogue is to be a Bet Midrash – a 'house of study.'" Rabbis must be "leaders who are teachers... who care." Study in most synagogues was, if anything, a marginal function, since the role of the rabbi as a teacher – especially for adults – was not part of most rabbis' job description.

- The job of a rabbi is to "create a community of people whom the rabbi cares about and who care about each other." While there was nothing new about the idea of a rabbi possessing a caring personality, the notion of a rabbi creating a caring community was revolutionary. Creating a community of carers – not just the rabbi as the "professional carer" – was also new.

---

studying." "Oh no," she said. "I read about you in *Time* and I just wanted to come and take a look." As she walked out, the rabbi reacted in mock surprise, which was followed by two minutes of laughter by all of us – including Rabbi Riskin. We were on the map!

LSS groundbreaking, June 30, 1968. Rabbi Riskin is second from left.
Credit: LSS archives.

Lincoln Square groundbreaking, June 30, 1968. Credit: LSS archives.

- "A God who loves must give commands." In the Jewish world generally, and the Orthodox Jewish world in particular, God's love was not spoken of openly. Christianity focused on the concept of God and love to such an extent that rabbis were afraid to speak of it lest they sound like Christian preachers.[10]

- "Orthodox Judaism… is a living religion…. There is room for interpretation…." Conventional wisdom in 1971 was that Orthodox Judaism was moribund, inflexible, and unsuited to modernity. Most Orthodox sources would have been hesitant to talk about "room for interpretation."

- "Ritual observances are important… because they fulfill our transcendental needs…. Our lives require an element of poetry." It would have been rare for an Orthodox congregational rabbi in 1971 to use the term "transcendental needs,"[11] and even rarer still to hear Jewish ritual observance equated with poetry.

- "God loves us no matter how guilty we are." Although this concept is, of course, a major theme in Judaism, emphasized especially in the theology of the holidays of Rosh Hashana and Yom Kippur, it was, oddly enough, rarely the message that was conveyed by Orthodox

---

[10] The *Time* article mentions that Steven Riskin, during the time he spent in Israel after college, sought out Martin Buber, "whose works he had been reading since he was twelve." Rabbi Riskin is quoted as respectfully disagreeing with Buber: "Buber gave us a theology, but not a lifestyle." Rabbi Riskin, in a conversation with me, added that he felt that Buber's understanding of God's love was closer to Christianity than to Judaism. In any case, *Time's* quoting Rabbi Riskin's "respectful disagreement" with Buber placed Rabbi Riskin, for the knowledgeable reader, in august company.

[11] It is probably no coincidence that Rabbi Riskin chose to use the word "transcendental" to the *Time* interviewer, because Transcendental Meditation (TM) and its ideologue Maharishi Mahesh Yogi were all the rage in the United States in 1971. Rabbi Riskin, even in his interview with *Time,* may have been reaching out to so many of the young Jews who were enamored of TM in 1971.

Judaism. What usually came through foremost was the guilt without the love.

- "Jews today... are giving the soul its due." Actually, this was wishful thinking. But with Rabbi Riskin, it became a self-fulfilling prophecy.

Reinterpreting Orthodox Judaism

An amazing transformation took place within the congregation regarding the general reaction to the word "Orthodox" and the concept of Orthodox Judaism. When Rabbi Riskin first assumed the pulpit at Lincoln Square, this word and concept carried with it a great deal of negative baggage. Rabbi Riskin was successful in communicating over the years the message – perhaps because he did not belabor Orthodox Judaism as a movement or as a set of standards – that Orthodox Judaism was not out of touch with the needs of modern Jews. On the contrary, Rabbi Riskin demonstrated that Orthodox Judaism was the most modern of Judaism's movements.[12] His message was that because of Orthodox Judaism's commitment to the details of Halacha and their application, it had a great deal to say about contemporary matters. It was his intention to show that Orthodox Judaism was in fact more relevant than the other streams of Judaism, which claimed relevance but did not use a well developed mechanism such as Halacha to apply Jewish concepts to contemporary matters.

---

[12] In this, Rabbi Riskin was prophetic. Hardly anyone in the mid-1960s was convinced that Orthodox Judaism could remake its image and celebrate a rebirth. It has already been cited that Conservative Judaism was seen as the truly *American* movement. It would be extremely difficult to demonstrate conclusively that Rabbi Riskin, in fact, was the prime mover of the Orthodox renaissance. However, my work on this book has given me the empirical sense that this is true. At any rate, Orthodox Judaism today has shed its image of being old-fashioned and out-of-step with the times, which was its greatest perceived liability in the 1960s.

Lincoln Square Synagogue. Credit: LSS archives.

❧ 6 ❧

REVITALIZING ADULT JEWISH EDUCATION

THE TIME IS LONG OVERDUE to re-evaluate the function of the Rabbi. A rabbi is a teacher of Jewish tradition, but a teacher who must create his own students if Judaism is to survive the twentieth century. The rabbi must inspire his student-congregants to learn. He must be thoroughly at home in the classical texts of Jewish tradition, but must communicate their spirit as well as their meaning to the past.

He must teach the faith without which the Bible becomes ancient mythology and the Talmud a branch of logic. He must attempt to vitalize the practice which is the expression of that faith.

– Rabbi Riskin[1]

When Rabbi Riskin wrote this letter to *Judaism* magazine in 1970, he was delivering an important message. First and foremost, Rabbi Riskin explained, a rabbi should function as a teacher and concurrently as a teacher-inspirer. As Rabbi Riskin outlined in the same letter quoted above, the American Jews' conception of a rabbi was defined and evaluated in terms of his ability to fulfill the roles of: "executive director, preacher, fund-raiser, social organizer, pastoral religious counselor, blessings dispenser at rites of passage and politician par excellence...."

It was not that Rabbi Riskin deemed the above functions unimportant. After all, the rabbi was an excellent preacher and a sought-after counselor,

---

[1] Letter from Rabbi Riskin to *Judaism* magazine, quoted by him in his Shavuot message, "Lincoln Square Synagogue Bulletin," June, 1970, 7.

and he became a very effective fundraiser. He was also a skilled "diplomat" among his congregants and community members. Rather, his vehemence in the letter was directed at the multiplicity of functions that were expected of a rabbi, because he added, "It is my experience that most rabbis fulfill this latter [Jack-of-all-trades] function, and consequently 'turn off' most of the young people, as well as the more intellectual and sensitive older people." In addition, he was horrified that while mastery of Jewish texts was central to a rabbi's training, "his textual training was hardly relevant to his professional requirements."

Rabbi Riskin firmly believed that he had to reach out to his congregation as an educator and inspirer. In his mind, his only hope of attracting marginally affiliated Jews to Jewish observance and the spiritual fulfillment embodied therein was to immerse them in Jewish texts and thought. He could not reasonably expect Jews to commit to a Jewish tradition of which they had little knowledge, or in which they had little interest.

When Rabbi Steven Riskin assumed the pulpit of Lincoln Square Synagogue in 1964, he was confronted with an enormous challenge. He was surrounded by a group of people who already had an agenda, and, in virtually all of the cases, that agenda did not include Torah study. Furthermore, his congregants did not express or define their Jewishness in terms of Torah. Their Jewishness expressed itself either in Jewish liberal politics, identification with Israel, or – most often – some vague sense that part of their identity was Jewish, without taking the time or trouble to try to isolate and understand that part of their identity. Samuel C. Heilman, in his study of typical Modern Orthodox synagogues in those days, notes:

> In practice… relatively few attend the regular weekly formal study groups which the shul and other Orthodox institutions sponsor…. This neglect… seems to stand as blatant evidence of an unconscionable disparity between principles of belief and realities of practice: by sponsoring and organizing formal study groups, the congregation displays its adherence to doctrine; by low attendance levels, members display their deviance from that doctrine.

Accordingly, the group continually calls for new classes, which disintegrate when relatively few persons attend....[2]

It was Rabbi Riskin's goal to encourage his congregants to rediscover their Jewish identity through Torah study, which, according to sociologist M. Herbert Danzger, is a "major portal of return" to Judaism for formerly disaffected Jews. Danzger observes that:

> Judaism lays immense stress on the study of the religious literature. To preserve Jewish life, which was disrupted by national exile and persecution, Judaism has built a homeland in the mind, a body of literature dealing with the minutest aspects of religious life and its social context, which permits those familiar with it to judge the world by its perspectives and practices. *Study and scholarship are essential elements of Judaism.*[3] [emphasis mine]

Shabbat Services

From the day Rabbi Riskin arrived at Lincoln Square, he created an atmosphere of inquiry, study, and intellectualism. One example of the novelty of Rabbi Riskin's approach can be seen in his attitude towards the Torah reading on Shabbat morning. It is common in synagogues for the Torah portion of the week to be read by a *ba'al koreh*, a reader who has prepared himself for the task. The portion is read entirely in Hebrew, chanted according to the traditional cantillation, or musical system. In most synagogues, the rabbi bases his sermon, or *derasha*, on some part of the content of the portion. Rabbi Riskin pointed out to his congregation that in ancient times, according to the original institution, the Torah reading was conducted in the spirit of *Talmud Torah be-rabim,* public Torah study. In fact, he recounted, during a certain period in Jewish history, there was an individual called the *meturgeman,* who would translate each Torah verse into Aramaic, the vernacular of the time, and explain it.

---

[2] Samuel C. Heilman, *Synagogue Life: A Study in Symbolic Interaction.* Chicago: University of Chicago Press, 1973, 222–223.

[3] Danzger, *Returning to Tradition,* 4–5.

Soon after he assumed the pulpit at LSS, Rabbi Riskin decided that he would transform the "rote" reading into a meaningful study session, and revived the *meturgeman* institution in a modern context. Between each of the sections (usually seven) which were read by the *ba'al koreh*, he would present a question on the Torah reading that was asked or implied by the traditional commentaries, and would extrapolate from the answer a meaningful idea. Rabbi Riskin's adaptation of the *meturgeman* style transformed what essentially would have been a prolonged period of Hebrew reading, incomprehensible to virtually everybody in the congregation, into a meaningful, intellectual, and spiritual experience.[4]

More importantly, this practice created an atmosphere of open inquiry and intellectual discourse, in which Jews were actively encouraged to ask questions about concepts in Judaism. Once Lincoln Square congregants realized that not only was asking questions permitted but also praiseworthy, their curiosity was piqued and they wanted to know more.

Rabbi Riskin's sermons, which usually dealt with the Torah portion of the week, were dramatic and passionate. He would apply the words of the Torah to a contemporary situation or, more frequently, to a question of inner religious development. Sometimes, Rabbi Riskin would discuss a topic in connection with the week's portion that related to an aspect of Jewish law and practice. Since the majority of the congregants were not strictly

---

[4] While it is true that the synagogues provided Hebrew Bibles (*Chumashim*) with an English translation, accompanied by some English commentary, the reading of the often arcane text in a stilted translation without a full explanation frequently left the reader cold. This was the widespread situation in virtually all synagogues at the time.

Following Rabbi Riskin's innovation in adapting the *meturgeman* style of reading the Torah, I have used this approach in synagogue services where I officiated. I found that in addition to the value of explaining several difficult points of the portion, my discussion of topics related to the Torah reading provided a certain rhythm to the service, and kept it from "dragging." Ironically, the Torah service on Shabbat morning, which was originally intended to be the focal point of the service, with communal participation in Torah study, ultimately became the most "boring" part of the service. The Torah reading was long, read in Hebrew, and there was no singing to liven it up. Rabbi Riskin's practice changed all of that.

observant of Jewish law, Rabbi Riskin demonstrated courage in tackling those aspects of Jewish life that were not being observed by his members.

> I would take a Halachic theme and try to show how relevant it is, in terms of human life[5].... What I tried to show was that Halacha was not "Mathematics 613."[6]

Rabbi Riskin would also discuss in his sermons the importance of combining secular studies with Jewish education, which was the cornerstone of Yeshiva University's philosophy. When confronted with the question of why it was crucial for a modern Jew to have a broad general education, Rabbi Riskin did not offer the response that was – and still is – given by so many others in the Orthodox Jewish world; namely, that secular studies are a "necessary evil" in order to earn a decent livelihood. Rabbi Riskin explained that he had a difficult time defining "secular studies." It all depends, the rabbi would state, on a person's perspective. He would often give the example of the study of biology. Is the study of biology a secular pursuit? he would ask. If one considers the study of biology to be the exploration of the greatness and complexity of the human being which God created, then biology is anything but a secular subject – it actually could be seen as the most religious of all subjects, since God is being celebrated as the Creator of wonders. The same way of thinking can be applied to other "secular" subjects.

---

[5] I recall that in 1972, on the Shabbat of *Parashat Achrei Mot,* Rabbi Riskin chose as his text the verse dealing with a woman's ritual impurity after her menstrual period. He explained the necessity of her immersing herself in a *mikveh* (ritual bath) before she and her husband could resume sexual relations. I don't remember what homiletic lesson he derived from the text, but I do recall his exhorting the married couples in the congregation to observe the laws of family purity. I remember noting to myself then what a bold decision it was to talk about this subject – which was rarely discussed openly in those days, and even more rarely in mixed audiences – and to preach its observance to what was still only a partially observant congregation.

[6] The number refers to the 613 commandments that a Jew is required to observe.

Rabbi Riskin made it abundantly clear that Torah study was part of the synagogue's *raison d'être,* and that as much spirituality would flow from the texts as it would from the traditional prayer services. Rabbi Riskin recalls that while synagogues traditionally appealed for money during *Kol Nidrei* (the Yom Kippur Evening Service), he made an appeal for hours of Torah study instead. Jesse Cogan, an early LSS member and an advertising and public relations professional, recalls:

> We created a special kind of an appeal card.... It was printed and I remember the headline, it said, "Rabbi Riskin would like you to make a commitment that won't cost you a penny."

It could be said that Rabbi Riskin's early background helped him understand how to break the cycle which, in so many synagogues, resulted in "teaching down" to the congregation. The ability to teach texts with love was significant in making Rabbi Riskin a *different* kind of rabbi, and may explain why so many of his early congregants use the word "charisma" when describing his personality. Shirley Wald reflects on that special quality:

> He is a spark. He was the pied piper from the very, very beginning. He was exciting, he was thrilling; his language was exciting, his physical dynamics.

Rabbi Riskin was determined not to fall into the trap of seeing – and, therefore, presenting – Judaism as a *list* of the 613 *mitzvot,* or commandments, that a Jew must observe. Once again, Rabbi Riskin had a nuanced view of the commandments that was rarely seen in the Orthodox world. While he strongly believed that Jews are required to observe the commandments, he avoided the common approach of viewing them as a "checklist" to be accomplished. On the contrary, he made Jewish observance, as expressed by the commandments, seem so stimulating and engrossing that his congregants and members of the general public who attended his sermons and lectures couldn't wait until their next encounter with him to be challenged even further.

Daniel Besdin, the son of the late Rabbi Morris Besdin, was a relative latecomer to LSS, only becoming a member in the late 1970s, but he expressed so well what many of the earlier congregants felt:

> I remember waking up, realizing it was Shabbat morning, and looking forward – there was sort of a little thrill – Oh, it's Shabbat morning, it's time for *shul*, and something's going to be happening....

Adult Education Institute

Soon after Rabbi Riskin assumed the pulpit of Lincoln Square, he established what he called the "Adult Education Institute," which, as a result of a substantial donation, became the Joseph Shapiro Institute of Jewish Studies.[7] The Institution began in 1965 with two classes by Rabbi Riskin on Wednesday evenings. The first class at 8:20 p.m. was on "The Art of Reading Hebrew," and was followed at 9 p.m. by "The Ideas and Personalities Which Founded Our Faith."

From the beginning, Rabbi Riskin's lectures were packed – first in the small synagogue room at 150 West End Avenue, which could accommodate about one hundred people, and later, from 1971 onwards, in the sanctuary of the new building at 200 Amsterdam Avenue, which held five hundred people. There were also an additional two hundred to three hundred people who listened to the classes, which were broadcast electronically to the ballroom downstairs. As the Joseph Shapiro Academy (later renamed the Joseph Shapiro Institute) developed, expanding to many classes with many teachers, virtually all of the classes were well-attended and popular.[8] Since

---

[7] It was actually Joseph Shapiro's widow, Bess, who donated money to the Institute. Her daughter married Moses Feuerstein, the scion of one of the few very wealthy Orthodox families in the US at that time. Bess Shapiro was confined to a wheelchair, and Vicky Riskin recalls sitting with the architects of the new building on Amsterdam Avenue to arrange wheelchair access for Mrs. Shapiro.

[8] Since so much at Lincoln Square radiated from Rabbi Riskin, the question of a cultic culture arises. Rabbi Riskin insists that he always tried hard not to let that culture prevail. Whether he was entirely successful in that attempt is open to debate,

the institute did not have a large budget, it could not hire well-known teachers, but it engaged young teachers who seemed to have great potential.

Classes were offered in a wide range of subjects, including modern and biblical Hebrew, Yiddish, Bible study, Jewish history (taught by Rabbi Riskin's "General Studies Rebbe," Professor Louis H. Feldman), Jewish law, Jewish thought, and even such modern topics such as Judaism and vegetarianism. In addition, Talmud was taught at the elementary, intermediate, and advanced levels, and five courses were given in "The Arts," including an extremely popular one taught by Peter Abelow called "Jewish Living Laboratory." In this course, Abelow taught people how to sing Zemirot (Shabbat table songs), and recite the Kiddush (the prayer over wine inaugurating Shabbat) and Havdala (the Shabbat valedictory prayer, also over wine).[9]

જી જી

In November 1969, the following advertisement appeared in the "Lincoln Square Synagogue Bulletin." It is hard to imagine these words appearing in any other synagogue bulletin. The headlines of the ad read:

We proudly but regretfully announce that the
Joseph Shapiro Academy of Jewish Studies
Must close registration for the Fall Term
in all but the Thursday Classes
Due to the overwhelming [sic] large response.

The body of the ad also provided a full list of the twelve classes that were available, and the days and times. At the bottom, the ad, conveying the

---

but that he tried is evident in his insistence on broadening the base of teachers in the Joseph Shapiro Academy beyond himself.
[9] Rabbi Riskin recalls his realization of the need to provide for the various different levels that began to develop in the synagogue. Very few – if any – institutions of Jewish learning at that time would contain in their curriculum a course in advanced Talmud on the one hand and a workshop on how to recite the Kiddush on the other.

excitement that filled the classes, urged those "closed out" of classes to plan ahead:

> Please register now for the Spring Term.
> Experience the joy of Torah study and learn
> in depth the glories of our heritage. At the very
> least, thrill with us at the myriads of College
> and Graduate Students who, along with our
> own members, flock to LSS to study Torah.[10]

Astonishingly, the classes were not only filled with loyal Lincoln Square members, but also non-members from the Jewish public at large. What brought these "myriads" from beyond the scope of the synagogue membership or even the Upper West Side?[11] After all, they did not have the advantage of the special atmosphere of inquiry created by Rabbi Riskin during the Shabbat service, and there were plenty of other lectures on Jewish topics taking place throughout the New York area.

To answer this question, we must go back to Lenore Brown's description of Lincoln Square as a "happening." The classes, particularly the Wednesday evening lectures, were wildly popular not only because of their academic content. There was a sense of spirituality, and the large crowds helped create an atmosphere of import. People sat on the edges of their seats as they waited for the young, energetic rabbi to begin speaking. Many students, men and women from Yeshiva University and the Jewish

---

[10] A difficult problem arose in relation to the "outside" people who packed the classes. Members became upset that space was being taken up by people who otherwise had nothing to do with the synagogue, and often there was no room left for members, even active ones. (See Chapter 10 for a further discussion on this topic.) Confronted with this problem, Rabbi Riskin had a hard time turning anyone away from Torah study. To my knowledge, this problem – one unprecedented in modern synagogue life – was never fully resolved.

[11] Although there are no figures on this, a number of people from the "outside," motivated and inspired by the classes, moved to the community and joined the synagogue.

Theological Seminary, who were already studying intensely about Judaism in their institutions, flocked to the Joseph Shapiro Academy.[12]

Robert Bersson was in dental school at New York University when he first began attending the Wednesday evening lectures in 1969. He recalls his excitement:

> I had attended yeshiva all of my life – including Yeshiva University – and had been raised in an Orthodox home, but I had never heard these current issues addressed. They were presented in an intellectually challenging way. These issues were relevant. There was content and there was inspiration.

As Rabbi Riskin taught, there was a sense that the very material that one was learning was a cause for celebration. His lectures were fascinating, thought-provoking, and deeply absorbing, and his preparation for his own classes was impeccable. Even in the Wednesday night lecture, which was the most topical, the rabbi consistently based himself on classical Jewish texts and their commentaries. Perhaps in doing so, he was applying Rabbi Besdin's method of teaching "It," the text, as opposed to teaching "about it." Of course, Rabbi Riskin's own interpretations featured heavily in the presentation, but the students absorbed the power of tradition by being shown, over and over, the derivation of laws and practices as they arose from ancient sources. While some students in the packed room were spellbound as they stared at the rabbi delivering his lecture, most took copious notes – another indication that participants were eager to remember and internalize not only the message, but the sources upon which it was built. A kind of reenactment of Sinai was taking place, just as the Rabbis said

---

[12] I was studying at Yeshiva University in the beginning years of the JSI, first for my undergraduate degree and then for my Master's and rabbinic ordination. Even though a good part of my day at YU was spent studying Talmud, I never missed Rabbi Riskin's class in Advanced Talmud on Thursday evenings. It was somehow different. His presentation was crystal clear. At the end of Rabbi Riskin's Talmud class, I always left with the feeling – which could not always be said of my classes at YU – that I had just been through a religious experience.

it should when Torah is studied.[13] The message at Sinai was delivered millennia ago amidst thunder and lightning to quaking listeners, and, here in Manhattan, it was taught, once again, cloaked in drama with gripping phrases and emotional stories. In a certain way, it was religious Jewish theater at its best.

THE WEDNESDAY EVENING LECTURES
The Teachings of Rabbi Soloveitchik

The evolution of topics for the hugely popular Wednesday evening lectures is interesting to note. At the beginning, the titles of the courses bore a strong resemblance to the typical adult education courses one would find in any synagogue. In the spring semester of 1965, Rabbi Riskin taught "The Ideas and Personalities which Founded Our Faith." But by fall 1966, the first class of the evening was "Understanding the Prayer Book," taught by Rabbi Riskin, and the second class of the evening was called "Contemporary Jewish Thought: Rav Kook and Rabbi J.B. Soloveitchik." In 1966, even in New York City, it would have been very difficult to find any class or lecture in which the thought of Rabbi Soloveitchik was being presented in a systematic way. Ironically, even at Yeshiva University, *where Rabbi Soloveitchik was in residence*, no actual courses were given – by him or by anyone else – in his thought.[14]

---

[13] *Avot de-Rabbi Natan* 1:6.

[14] This is partly because Rabbi Soloveitchik, in the context of his life at Yeshiva University, primarily saw himself as a teacher of Talmud, not of philosophy. No one at YU in those years would have even presumed to talk about "Rabbi Soloveitchik's thought." By the 1960s, he had published only a few articles and essays, all in Hebrew. In addition to his Talmud classes, he gave regular philosophical lectures in memory of his father in Yiddish, and later in memory of his mother and his wife in English, but the notes on these lectures were not published until the 1980s, twenty years after Rabbi Riskin began transmitting this material to students! The 1990s and our current decade saw – and continue to see – large numbers of works which contain "reconstituted" material from Rabbi Soloveitchik.

Rabbi Riskin's brand-new approach of reaching out to the unaffiliated and not-yet-committed required the support of a highly respected theoretician if it was to have substance and credibility. Rabbi Riskin made Rabbi Soloveitchik his theoretician. In addition to explaining Rabbi Soloveitchik's thinking on halachic existentialism, Rabbi Riskin frequently introduced a point – in a class or in a sermon – by saying, "According to my Rebbe, Rav Soloveitchik…" The early Lincoln Square congregants were not intimately familiar with the centrality of the student-teacher relationship in Judaism. By frequently mentioning the ideas and practices which he had adopted from his teacher, Rabbi Soloveitchik, Rabbi Riskin helped solidify this concept in the mind of the people.[15]

In addition, Rabbi Riskin's frequent quotations, citations, and courses on Rabbi Soloveitchik's unique understanding of Judaism[16] transformed the congregation of Lincoln Square Synagogue into one of the first congregations to live the Rav's approach.[17]

---

[15] There was a growing cadre of students from the JSS program of Yeshiva University who considered Rabbi Riskin as their rebbe. Rabbi Riskin was therefore creating a chain linking these students, who were new to Torah, to Rabbi Soloveitchik. Although it didn't work in exactly the same way with Rabbi Riskin's Lincoln Square "students" (because they were not exactly students in the formal sense), everyone in Lincoln Square knew of Rabbi Soloveitchik, and respected him as Rabbi Riskin's teacher, even if they never saw or met him.

[16] A complete analysis of Rabbi Soloveitchik's philosophy and approach to Halacha is far beyond the scope of this book. However, the essential notion, which Rabbi Soloveitchik develops in his work *Halachic Man*, of Jewish Law being the source and the reflection of Jewish philosophy and Jewish creativity, is the central concept which pervaded Lincoln Square Synagogue. Halacha was *never* explained by Rabbi Riskin as a list of dos and don'ts; it was always put forth as expected actions (or non-actions, for the "don'ts) for which the payoff would be a deeper understanding of human beings, God, and oneself. In a way, Lincoln Square Synagogue was a laboratory in which Rabbi Riskin translated Rabbi Soloveitchik's thinking into practice for his congregation.

[17] The other would have been the congregation formed around the Maimonides School in Brookline, Massachusetts, which was founded by Rabbi Soloveitchik and

The Holocaust

In 1972, Rabbi Riskin took a dramatic curricular step, presenting a series of lectures entitled "The Theological Implications of the Holocaust." In the early 1970s, the extremely sensitive area of theology of the Holocaust was hardly being touched, especially in the Orthodox world. Richard Rubenstein had written his work *After Auschwitz* in 1966, in which he made radical statements about the end of the covenant between God and the Jewish people. A statement by Emil Fackenheim in 1968, which Rabbi Riskin quoted often, spoke about the absolute necessity of Jewish life continuing after the Holocaust "so as not to grant Hitler a posthumous victory."[18] However, neither of these early "Holocaust theologians" were Orthodox; it was an area full of landmines for the traditional believer. Orthodox Rabbi Eliezer Berkovits published his *Faith after the Holocaust* only in 1973, and Rabbi Irving Greenberg, an Orthodox rabbi and historian, did not publish his extremely controversial essay on Holocaust theology, "Cloud of Smoke, Pillar of Fire: Judaism, Christianity, and Modernity after the Holocaust" until 1974.[19] But Rabbi Riskin, himself troubled for years by questions about God and the Holocaust,[20] realized that there was no way that a searching Jew in the post-Holocaust generation could possibly consider the question of belief without confronting the theological implications of the Holocaust head-on. So, even before Berkovits and Greenberg, Rabbi Riskin took the step, once

---

directed for many years by his wife, Tonya Lewit Soloveitchik. Rabbi Soloveitchik was in regular attendance there and functioned as that congregation's "rabbi."

[18] Emil L. Fackenheim, *To Mend the World: Foundations of Post-Holocaust Thought*. Bloomington, IN: Indiana University Press, 1994, 299–300.

[19] When Rabbi Riskin spoke about the Holocaust in subsequent years, after Berkovits and Greenberg had published their works, he would refer to their ideas, but back in 1972, he tackled this most difficult of all subjects "on his own."

[20] Rabbi Riskin, in a conversation with me, said that preparing this Holocaust course helped him to deal with his own questions of post-Holocaust faith, and indicated that this was the case with a number of topics that he taught. It occurs to me that this may be teaching at its best, as opposed to the more commonly assumed model of the teacher, who is confident in his subject, and is overflowing with information.

again before huge crowds hanging on his every word, into the dangerous but important waters of theodicy, the positing of a God of good in a world of evil.

The Holocaust lectures brought about a greater awareness within the synagogue of the majesty and dignity of faith in the face of unanswerable questions. Rabbi Riskin did not believe in a "broken covenant" between God and Israel. There were periods of *hester panim*, to be sure, in which God hid His face and His actions became inscrutable, but the covenant still stood. More radical theologians might question the simplicity of such an unshakable doctrine of faith, but somehow the rabbi's expression of faith, belief, and especially practice in the face of tragedy always seemed anything but simple. Even when Rabbi Riskin spoke "critically" of God's actions, it was clear that his criticism was addressed to a Being whose existence was eternal and whose relationship with His nation was deep and abiding.[21]

The Six Day War and Rabbi Riskin's Messianism

Rabbi Riskin had always presented to his congregants and students many traditional Jewish texts which discussed the concept of redemption. In June of 1967, an actual "workshop" in redemption had presented itself on the world scene – Israel's Six Day War. During this war, Rabbi Riskin focused on directing the eyes of his congregation to God's controlling Hand in the miraculous victory and its redemptive implications.

---

[21] Rabbi Riskin likes what Ari Goldman said about him in his book *The Search for God at Harvard*. Goldman writes about Rabbi Riskin, "…[H]e could see the problems created by Orthodoxy's clash with the modern world, but his answers fell back on old, tired ways" (Ari L. Goldman, *The Search for God at Harvard,* New York: Random House, 1991, 216). Although Goldman's words are not exactly complimentary, Rabbi Riskin feels that they described him well. From his perspective, it is not up to a contemporary rabbi to create a new theology to respond to new problems; it is rather a rabbi's responsibility to show how traditional thinking can be relevant to modern situations. This position explains well, for example, the difference between Rabbi Riskin's thinking on the Holocaust and that of Rabbi Irving Greenberg.

Over and over again, with even more energy and verve than usual, the rabbi would refer to the period as *ikveta de-meshicha*, the "footsteps of the Messiah." Sitting in Lincoln Square Synagogue, far away from the Israeli battlefield and the victory celebrations in Jerusalem and Tel Aviv, his students and congregants listened rapturously as Rabbi Riskin told stories of miracles during the war, proclaiming this victory as a huge step toward redemption. One could actually sense the arrival of a new world filled with the spirit of God.

Within the walls of Lincoln Square Synagogue, redemption had seemed near. Even though the complete redemption, in the form of the Messiah, did not take place, the concept of pre-redemption pervaded the consciousness and lives of Lincoln Square people in those days, weeks, and months. Of course, Jews around the world stood in wonder of the marvelous victory. Jews at Lincoln Square did, too, but they also experienced redemption in the same way that Jews on Passover night experience the redemption from Egypt – as if it had truly happened to them.

Issues of the Day

Most rabbis – then and now – try to deal with contemporary topics. Rabbi Riskin, however, was one of the few rabbis to search out halachic implications based upon current events. His full curriculum for the Wednesday evening lectures was remarkably broad and groundbreaking.

In 1971, he spoke about issues of the day, including birth control and abortion. He also tackled sensitive Jewish issues, such as the case for abolishing the second day of major Jewish holidays as Reform Judaism had done. (The "second day" was established because of a problem in ascertaining the exact date of the holiday in ancient times. However, the traditional legal codifiers insisted that it be preserved.) Rabbi Riskin opposed canceling the second day, and supplied thoughtful reasons for its preservation.

Rabbi Riskin dealt with another subject which, though not as central to contemporary debate, was nonetheless interesting – the revival of the

Sanhedrin, the ancient Jewish Court. Rabbi Riskin used his presentation on this rather arcane issue to raise sensitive questions regarding the changeability of Jewish law and practice.

In 1973, Rabbi Riskin presented a long list of contemporary topics concerning which he found an element of Halacha to discuss. The list, under the rubric of "Issues of the 'Now' Generation," included such topics as:

- Contemporary creativity within the Halachic process

- Attitudes toward Oriental religions

- Homosexuality, pornography, and other "victimless crimes"

- Penology and Attica, affirmative action and American political issues

- The Lansky case, Neturei Karta, returning the liberated lands to the Arabs and their sale to Jews

- The Chief Rabbinate, Aliyah

- The media and Watergate

- The feminist movements

While it might seem ludicrous to claim to deal with such broad topics in a serious way in the context of once-a-week lectures, the point was not so much to cover the subjects extensively from the perspective of each of their fields – psychology, sociology, politics – but rather, to demonstrate that Jewish law and Jewish thought had something relevant and important to say on each of these contemporary matters.[22] In this way, Rabbi Riskin could

---

[22] Rabbi Riskin's material, if somewhat popularized, always had a scholarly air, with sources which the capable and interested student could research (I did, many times). The more popular rabbinic approach involved a far more vague application of the so-called Jewish *attitude* toward contemporary events and problems. Rabbi Riskin never claimed expertise in any discipline other than Halacha and Jewish thought. Unlike other rabbis of the time, he did not present a facile, unrealistic solution to a complex problem. Rather, he presented Jewish sources which helped define the problem, perceive the complexity, and look toward possible (perhaps multiple)

accomplish his ultimate goal of permanently removing the stain of irrelevance in people's perception of Orthodox Judaism.

Lectures on Love and Sexuality

Rabbi Riskin had succeeded in transforming Torah study into a spiritual activity, and spurred on by the positive response he received, he developed a seemingly endless succession of topics for these Wednesday evening lectures. But there is one topic which stands out in the memories of Lincoln Square members and course attendees. In June, 1967, the "Lincoln Square Synagogue Bulletin" published a review of the past semester's classes, noting that:

> The younger element showed great interest in the later lecture in which Rabbi Riskin discussed Jewish attitudes toward pre-marital and post-marital love and sex.

If Lincoln Square Synagogue represented a revolution, then the Love and Sex course, which began in the fall of 1979 was a revolution within a revolution. Rabbi Riskin says that he made the decision to tackle this topic because he saw how casually sex was being treated at that time. Against the backdrop of the 1960s and 1970s, with their huge upheaval in attitudes toward love, sex and feminism, Rabbi Riskin took his students on a journey to the very essence of human sexuality from the textual point of view. He chose as his starting point not the societal viewpoint of these decades, nor the sexual prohibitions inherent in Halacha, but rather the very creation of man and woman at the beginning of time, as presented by the Torah.

Mindful of the fact that new and radical viewpoints about the origins and development of female and male sexuality were exploding all around him during that period, the rabbi navigated a course which did not ignore contemporary conceptions, but which showcased the text of Genesis and its exquisitely majestic narrative of man, woman, sexuality, temptation, sin, and

solutions. It goes without saying how much more appealing Rabbi Riskin's approach was to an academically-oriented audience.

forgiveness. The atmosphere in the room during these lectures was electric. The silent, expectant, and serious mood of the students packed into the synagogue indicated that the Jewish learners were looking to Rabbi Riskin as a source of as-yet-unrevealed knowledge about themselves. In fact, the rabbi was presenting to this diverse group of Jews nothing less than the narrative they shared with each other and with all other human beings. Rabbi Riskin was helping them to look beyond their identities as professionals, students, or parents, and to plumb the depths of their hearts to discover their sexual and human identity, the very stuff of which they were made.

Rabbi Riskin was not attempting to make the story of the origins of man and woman relevant to his audience by relating it to contemporary subjects, such as Jewish dating on the Upper West Side or finding one's mate. He would deal with these topics later on. Rather, he was enabling and empowering each individual in the room to feel the powerful impact of the Biblical text upon his or her very existence and his or her essential identity. Every male in that room became Adam, every woman Eve. Among the wider public, the lectures had such broad appeal that it attracted the likes of Dr. Ruth Westheimer — no stranger herself to the subject of sexuality — and John Lennon and Yoko Ono.

The wildly popular courses on love and sexuality created a construct for a meaningful process of dating and marriage within the newly burgeoning Modern Orthodox community on the Upper West Side. With the forming of the Lincoln Square Community around Rabbi Riskin, there arose what was probably the first youthful, newly-observant Modern Orthodox community in the history of the Jews in the United States.

The formation of this new type of community created a vacuum in certain areas of Jewish life, not the least of which was the question of how to find a compatible mate. Kashrut, Shabbat, Torah study — even in their complexity — were relatively attainable goals. You bought kosher food, you avoided the prohibitions of Shabbat and kept its positive commandments, you set aside time to study and took advantage of the absorbing classes being offered. But marriage was different. The newly observant had to set themselves new criteria in their search for life partners. Danzger notes that

"…the major problem [for newly observant people] may be finding someone to date, as they have not established the network of relations in the new community that gives rise to contacts."[23] Lincoln Square Synagogue may have been the first venue in the United States to provide – as a community – the opportunity for newly observant Jews to meet each other.[24]

The idea of an arranged marriage, or even of a marriage broker (*shadchan*) was, in those times, clearly relegated to the ultra-Orthodox world. On the other hand, simply "playing the field," as one would have done before becoming observant, was no longer possible.[25] The Wednesday evening

---

[23] Danzger, *Returning to Tradition,* 313–314.

[24] Rabbi Riskin's Wednesday evening lectures, which drew the biggest crowds, took on a social aspect as well. My mother, Anne Abramson, of blessed memory, who served as an officer of both the synagogue and its sisterhood at various times, took note of the continuing growth of the Wednesday evening attendance. She made the suggestion – which was accepted and even encouraged by Rabbi Riskin – that refreshments be served after the lecture so that male and female students might have a forum for socializing. While there are no exact figures, a number of engagements resulted from couples who met after a Wednesday evening lecture.

[25] Nowadays, most institutions for *ba'alei teshuva* take an active part in "fixing up" newly observant students with potential marriage partners. Depending on the particular institution, this is done either in a less or more formal way. If the institution is firmly in the Modern Orthodox camp, the "fix-up" might take the form of an invitation to a Shabbat meal for the young man and woman at the home of a rabbi or teacher, so that they can get acquainted and, if they wish, arrange a "date" themselves at a later point. In institutions that lean more in the direction of ultra-Orthodox, it is common for a couple to be set up on an official "date," which typically takes place in a formal setting over light refreshments. During the date, the couple ask each other preliminary questions with the intention of establishing by the end of the date whether there is potential for marriage.

In the days of Rabbi Riskin at Lincoln Square, this kind of operation, except perhaps in the most informal sense, would have been unheard of. Rabbi Riskin's approach – in this area as in so many others – was to help the student or congregant develop a sense of independence as well as the knowledge base and theoretical framework with which to make a proper decision *on his or her own*. Which approach is "better" (and what the criteria are for deciding) is a question left open.

lectures on love and sexuality provided a community setting and opened up new opportunities for dating in order to find one's future spouse.[26]

Marital Laws and Family Purity

Vicky Riskin offered a class for brides-to-be on the subject of "Marital Laws and Family Purity." The class, which was held in her home once a week, focused on the responsibility of the Jewish woman to observe the laws governing sexual relations with her husband. Since Jewish law decrees several days of sexual separation between husband and wife each month, the subject had to be handled carefully.

After all, many of the women in Vicky's class were hearing about these laws for the first time in their lives. The very nature of the subject matter required explicitness, but at the same time, it was crucial to demonstrate sensitivity. This was especially important for Vicky's students, who were of various levels of religious observance. Vicky made sure that in addition to teaching the intricacies of the marital laws, she offered some friendly and "motherly" advice about sex and marriage in general.

Both Vicky and Rabbi Riskin strongly believed that the ancient laws regarding family purity were deeply compatible with modern life and could even enhance a marriage. In the 1960s and 1970s, when sexual promiscuity was rampant, the idea that sexual separation could actually refresh a couple's sexual relationship was interesting and novel. Both Vicky in her classes and the rabbi in his lectures presented to their students the traditional Jewish sources that spoke of these laws as having the power to invigorate a marriage, and at the same time encouraged the couple to find ways to express their love and affection in a non-sexual way.

---

[26] While writing this book, I ran into an old acquaintance in Jerusalem, an American expatriate, who I did not know had any connection to Lincoln Square Synagogue. When I told him what I was writing about, he interrupted with, "Oh, yes, the Wednesday night classes. I met my wife there."

Rabbi Herschel Cohen

As Lincoln Square Synagogue began to increase in numbers and popularity and the educational programs continued to develop and expand, Rabbi Riskin found it increasingly difficult to focus on what he always believed to be one of the secrets of Lincoln Square's success – its daily "ritual operation." In order for the synagogue to function properly, the rabbi had to undertake many daily responsibilities. For example, he had to order ritual materials such as *tallitot* (prayer shawls), *kippot* (skullcaps), and prayer books for the various holidays. He also had to be make himself available so that his congregants could approach him with their questions in preparation for the upcoming holidays. As important as this day-to-day ritual maintenance of the synagogue was to Rabbi Riskin, he lacked the time and interest in administrative procedures to fulfill those functions properly and efficiently.

In 1967, just three years after Rabbi Riskin joined Lincoln Square Synagogue, he felt this pressure intensely and decided to make the first addition to the Lincoln Square Synagogue rabbinic/educational staff. That addition was Rabbi Herschel Cohen. Rabbi Riskin had first encountered Rabbi Cohen at the *bet midrash* (the communal study hall) at Yeshiva University and thought of him as being a "very trustworthy and responsible" individual. Although Rabbi Cohen had been ordained by Yeshiva University two years before Rabbi Riskin, Rabbi Cohen had decided that his future was in social work. When Rabbi Riskin approached Rabbi Cohen in 1967, asking him to join him at Lincoln Square Synagogue, Rabbi Cohen was working as a social worker in New York. He accepted Rabbi Riskin's offer and agreed to the title of Ritual Administrator.

Not only did Rabbi Cohen efficiently perform the tasks assigned to him, but he also endeared himself almost immediately to the congregation. Because he dealt so well with the day-to-day needs of the synagogue, people saw him as the first address for their needs.

An extremely direct individual with a wonderful, off-beat sense of humor, Rabbi Cohen began teaching in the Joseph Shapiro Academy. He taught courses in Basic Hebrew Reading, Basic Talmud, and – his favorite course – Basic Judaism, a curriculum he created himself which constituted a review of the all of the major philosophical points of Judaism, as well as the practical observance of rituals and holidays.

Rabbi Cohen possessed a deep understanding of Rabbi Riskin's spiritual vision for Lincoln Square Synagogue, and he carved out ways to promote that special approach in his own distinctive style. The areas of his involvement in the synagogue ran across the spectrum: In addition to the Joseph Shapiro classes mentioned, Rabbi Cohen took charge of the ever-growing number of prospective converts to Judaism who were referred to Lincoln Square by word of mouth for their studies. He and his wife, Shulie, who formed close bonds with the members of the congregation, regularly invited Hebrew School students and their families to Shabbat meals at their home, in Lincoln Towers. His loyal cadre of students over the years at Joseph Shapiro and successful converts with whom he had worked also frequently joined the Cohens for Shabbat.

One could certainly question how it was that such a talented and beloved individual could serve alongside Rabbi Riskin for all those years without feeling that he was in Rabbi Riskin's shadow. Although Rabbi Cohen had already left this world before interviews for this book began, it was clear to everyone – and became even clearer to the author after a conversation with Shulie – that Rabbi Cohen was so focused on his work at the synagogue and so respectful of what Rabbi Riskin had created, that such feelings were thoroughly foreign to him.

As Rabbi Riskin grew over the years in fame and national stature, he had even less time and patience for the day-to-day running of the synagogue. Rabbi Herschel Cohen, with his eye for detail, and his friendly demeanor, held the synagogue together throughout Rabbi Riskin's tenure and beyond.

Rejuvenating Orthodox Judaism

Never before in the history of Jews in America had Torah study been so available and inviting to Jews with little or no background in Jewish studies or observance. For the first time, the thinking and approach of the greatest living teacher in American Orthodoxy, Rabbi Joseph B. Soloveitchik, was made accessible to everyone. Ideas and principles that were presented in lectures began to appear in everyday conversations of Lincoln Square's community members. Lincoln Square Synagogue was alive every night of the week with Jews, young and old, trying to understand the ancient texts in their modern context.

A national newsmagazine had taken note of the phenomenon, thus conferring upon the synagogue a national iconic status. Orthodox Judaism could no longer be seen as out of step with the times. Rabbi Riskin had brought a new dignity to the phenomenon called Orthodox Judaism, a dignity long felt in the ivory tower of the *bet midrash* by learned students engaged in unraveling the mysteries of the Torah, but now, finally, experienced by the rank and file outside the walls of the yeshiva. For many who studied with him, their world and its priorities had changed: The Torah and its views became the measuring rod which evaluated society, and not vice versa.[27] Rabbi Riskin had indeed "created his own students," as he had charged all rabbis to do in his letter to *Judaism* in 1970.

---

[27] Rabbi Riskin loved to tell the story of the guide who was taking a group of American women through the Louvre Museum in Paris. As they stopped at each work of art, one outspoken woman would hold forth on the painting, saying that she really didn't understand what was so special about this or that creation. At one point, she even said, "I think my ten-year-old grandson could have painted something better than this one." The guide could take it no longer. Drawing himself up to his full height, his voice dripping with distaste, he said, "Madame, when you are touring the Louvre, it is not the Louvre that is on trial, it is *you*!" The rabbi's point, of course, was that even as one explores Judaism to decide if it is relevant for him or her, that person must stand in awe and respect of a profound tradition that has spanned the millennia. Once again, a fascinating balance in Rabbi Riskin's presentation of Judaism to the uninitiated – explore it, evaluate it for yourself, but stand in awe of it.

❧ 7 ❧

FAITH THROUGH PRAYER

IN HIS LETTER TO JUDAISM MAGAZINE in 1970, Rabbi Riskin stated in unequivocal terms that the rabbi "must teach the faith, without which the Bible becomes ancient mythology and the Talmud a branch of logic." But how does one teach faith? Virtually all institutions of Jewish learning in the United States until the mid-1960s had fallen into the same trap – rabbis and Jewish educators commonly and erroneously assumed that that their overarching responsibility was to teach Jewish texts and concepts to their students, and that faith would automatically follow.[1] This attitude may have been a throwback to the methods of European Jewish education of earlier years, where faith was imparted in the home and the surrounding Jewish society, and the question of the relevance of Judaism was never in doubt.

---

[1] It is true that some of the traditional yeshivot in America had a *mashgiach ruchani*, a spiritual adviser to the students. Of course, his effectiveness had a great deal to do with the extent of his understanding of how traditional Jewish learning and practice – and the faith that must accompany it – could be taught and inculcated on the American scene. At Yeshiva University, for example, in those years the *mashgiach ruchani* was a well-intentioned European rabbi with a sterling background in the European yeshiva world and a striking aura of holiness emanating from his face. Unfortunately, he did not speak English, and delivered his lectures on the spirituality of Torah study in Yiddish, a language that the majority of the students at YU did not understand! For many reasons, I always had a feeling of ineffable sadness when I heard him speak, related both to the honor of this obviously holy person and to the realization that the institution of *mashgiach ruchani* was not even beginning to serve its purpose.

But a society in which faith was automatically transmitted through one's environment no longer existed.

Many of the classical Jewish philosophers taught that belief in God was the result of an intellectual process and that God's existence could be "proved" through logic. For example, they argued, one need only observe the orderliness and the obvious "design" of the universe to realize that there exists a Designer.[2] Considering Rabbi Riskin's own deep commitment to intellectualism, one might have expected him to present to his congregants an intellectual approach to faith, such as the teleological argument described above. However, as committed to intellectualism as he was, Rabbi Riskin sensed that in order to teach a living, breathing faith to his Lincoln Square students, he had to go beyond the intellect.

Prayer

Prayer was the one area of Jewish life which involved not only faith, but a method of direct communication with the Divine. Rabbi Riskin recognized that the act of praying for the purpose of communicating with God had the enormous potential to inspire faith in those who had little connection to Judaism. Because there was no accepted curriculum for the teaching of faith, transmitting belief to Jews who lacked a Jewish background was no trivial task. It was therefore especially crucial to reveal the beauty of prayer to those just discovering Judaism. With all its intricate laws and nuanced strictures, the regimen of Orthodox observance could quickly fall by the wayside for a searching Jew if there was no faith to hold it in place. For that matter, it was unlikely that many Jews would even become interested in adopting an observant lifestyle without the enriching element of spirituality within Judaism.

Rabbi Riskin intensely believed in the power of personal prayer, and taught what the ancient rabbis said in their traditional texts – that through prayer a human being could reach out to God, and beg and supplicate Him

---

2 This is often referred to as "the teleological argument," deriving from the Greek *telos,* end.

for his daily needs, both physical and spiritual. Such direct and frequent interaction with the Divine had the power to inspire faith. Rabbi Riskin witnessed with his own eyes the bond that was forged between his grandmother and God as she intoned the prayers with deep concentration every Friday night.

Morton Landowne, a long-time Lincoln Square congregant and former president of the synagogue, recalls an incident which took place at a scheduled dialog between Rabbi Riskin and a representative of the Reconstructionist Movement. The dialog, which was part of a series of discussions between Rabbi Riskin and representatives of different streams of Judaism in America, took place at Lincoln Square on a Wednesday evening in the 1980s. The Reconstructionist representative had explained that Reconstuctionism does not predicate a belief in a personal God. A member of the audience wanted to know why the prayer for the sick is recited in Reconstructionist synagogues. To whom is this prayer addressed? Morton Landowne recalls the Reconstructionist's answer and Rabbi Riskin's reaction:

> [The Reconstructionist] said that [they recited the prayer] in order to inform the community that a member was not well and to let him know of the group's concern. Then he said, "I'm sure when Rabbi Riskin says [the prayer] he isn't thinking that an angel is going to come down and heal the person." Rabbi Riskin, to much laughter, was standing next to him vigorously nodding his head.

In twentieth-century America, if Jews were involved in any area of the Jewish religion, it was in the arena of prayer. Even if a Jewish person was not committed to regular synagogue attendance, that person was still likely to attend bar mitzvah ceremonies and perhaps High Holiday services. The overwhelming irony of it all was that although many Jews prayed, few, if any, were motivated by the idea that prayer was a means of direct communication with God. In fact, congregants in many synagogues viewed the services more as social gatherings than as opportunities for spiritual development.

In the 1960s and 1970s, this issue manifested itself in a prevalent and embarrassing practice – talking during the prayer service. This phenomenon, which had occurred throughout Jewish history, had been occurring in America for years, especially in most Orthodox synagogues. Sometimes the talking was so widespread and loud that a worshipper would actually miss parts of the service – the Cantor's repetition of the *Amidah,* which is the central prayer of the service, or the Torah reading, which was formulated in ancient times to insure that Jewish worshippers would also become familiar with the primary text of Judaism, the Five Books of Moses. Rabbis pleaded with their congregations in their sermons for silence during prayers, often to no avail. Some rabbis even insisted on pausing the service until the talking stopped, but that method was largely ineffective, since the interruption disrupted the flow of prayers and it wasn't long before the talking resumed.

All sorts of explanations were offered for this troubling phenomenon. The most popular justification was the claim that since Orthodox Jews feel so "at home" in the synagogue, they feel as relaxed and uninhibited in their speech as they would at home. Of course, this analogy was spurious and patently ridiculous because Halacha, Jewish law itself, prohibited casual conversation in the synagogue if it was not related to the task at hand – prayer.

The real explanation was simple. Most people spoke during the services because prayer was not compelling for them. Many people talked during the prayers because they did not understand their structure or underlying philosophy. People conversed out of boredom because they genuinely felt that what they had to say to their neighbor was far more interesting that what was "officially" happening in the synagogue.

To further exacerbate the problem of worshippers feeling disconnected from the prayer service, in many synagogues, a professional cantor would sing elaborate pieces of *chazzanut,* liturgical music, which, while often entertaining, did not succeed in communicating to a new generation a longing for God and the pathos of prayer. Most congregants were either unfamiliar with the Hebrew language or understood some Hebrew words yet lacked a conceptual understanding of the prayers being sung. Furthermore, the operatic cantors in these synagogues gave the congregants an excuse to remain passive during the prayer service.

Some (mainly Orthodox) synagogues without cantors would operate on a rotational basis, where able and knowledgeable congregants would volunteer to serve as prayer leaders. It was therefore very common in these synagogues for a different person to be leading the prayer service each time. While these "amateur cantors" were often sincere, frequently they were even less inspiring than the professionals.

As Rabbi Riskin considered how to reinvigorate the prayer service at Lincoln Square Synagogue, neither the typical professional cantor model nor the "amateur volunteer cantor" model was possible – or advisable. As for Rabbi Riskin himself, he felt that he could not very well lead the services. It would have been awkward for him to function as a rabbi and a cantor and besides, he did not possess a melodious voice.

Rabbi Riskin was looking for a cantor who would not only be competent in leading the services but who would also infuse spirituality into the prayers. Rabbi Riskin had been heavily influenced by the legendary Rabbi Shlomo Carlebach in his attitude toward spiritual prayer. In the 1960s, Shlomo Carlebach revolutionized and spiritualized Jewish music and brought many young Jews back to Judaism.[3] A musician and a follower of the Lubavitcher Rebbe, Rabbi Shlomo Carlebach brilliantly adapted the Chassidic *niggun* (tune) to the American ear and injected a high level of spirituality into his music. His personality was extremely extroverted and charismatic and he communicated, in stories and music, a message that was not being conveyed by other Jewish spiritual leaders: namely, that Judaism was, in fact, rich in spiritual content and meaning.

---

[3] A great deal more needs to be studied and said about Shlomo Carlebach and his influence. It is interesting to note that in his seminal work *American Judaism: A History*, from which I frequently quote in this book, Jonathan D. Sara devotes six pages to Shlomo Carlebach, while Rabbi Riskin and Lincoln Square are not mentioned at all. Perhaps this is because Carlebach was so radically countercultural, and therefore more conspicuous, while Rabbi Riskin and Lincoln Square were a mixture of counterculture and establishment (with new and different ideas, but nonetheless a synagogue with a Board of Directors and all the trimmings of the establishment), and therefore were less conspicuous.

Rabbi Riskin knew that he needed a cantor who was able to blend spirituality with music, like Carlebach, and who could do musically what he was doing verbally – to create the conditions within the synagogue for spirituality and, ultimately, the kind of religious experience which can inspire and result in faith. Rabbi Riskin found such a man in Sherwood Goffin.

Sherwood Goffin

Rabbi Riskin had known Sherwood Goffin for some time and had often worked with him at Yeshiva University youth events, where Rabbi Riskin would speak inspiring words of Torah which were accompanied by Sherwood's spiritual singing and guitar playing. Although Sherwood had previously held part-time cantorial positions, he was essentially a Jewish folk singer with a style borrowed partially from the folksongs of the 1960s and partially from traditional Jewish folk and cantorial melodies.[4] He was an extremely personable, kind, and intelligent person with a talent for creating a spiritual mood and connecting with people through words and music.

Sherwood was studying for a graduate degree in psychology at Yeshiva University and had married his wife Batya only the year before when Rabbi Riskin first offered him the position as cantor at Lincoln Square Synagogue. Although Sherwood was heavily occupied with his studies at the time and the salary being offered to him was meager and the prospects uncertain, Rabbi Riskin managed to persuade him to accept the position. Sherwood recalls that his initial reluctance and concerns soon gave way to enthusiasm.

> I knew Shlomo Riskin pretty well by then, and I knew anything he did
> would work. I didn't feel he was taking such a chance. I think I knew
> him well enough that if he was doing something, and he was
> committed to it – he said, "Sherwood, we're going to have one of the

---

[4] After assuming the position at Lincoln Square, Sherwood Goffin enrolled at Yeshiva University's Cantorial Training Institute, where he had already taken some undergraduate courses before he came to Lincoln Square. Sherwood felt that he owed it to Lincoln Square to become a credentialed professional. He received a cantorial degree from Yeshiva University.

biggest shuls in the United States." I knew he was going to make it into something special.

And so, in August 1965, Sherwood Goffin became Lincoln Square Synagogue's first cantor. Rabbi Riskin and Sherwood worked seamlessly as a team and the services took on a deep aura of spirituality. Sherwood Goffin was an emotional prayer leader, able to infuse the music of his prayers with that intense emotional energy. In effect, Cantor Goffin was also teaching the most profound message of prayer – sincerity. Perhaps most significantly, the cantor encouraged a great deal of congregational singing during the prayers. There was no doubt in anyone's mind that Sherwood was sincere when he stood at the prayer-podium. He was such a likable and warm personality "offstage" that no one doubted his absolute dedication when he was leading the congregation in prayer. We can hear the attachment Sherwood Goffin created to his special brand of prayer as we listen to Debbie Abelow, still speaking with emotion more than twenty years after having moved away from Lincoln Square:

> Sherwood I still miss to this day…. If you talk about how the *shul* affected us, we were definitely in love with the *davvening* [prayer service]. That was inspiring. It was just an emotional experience. I have not ever felt that since. I mean, you can have a very nice *Hazzan*, but it's not him.

Sherwood often used melodies from Jewish music popular at the time rather than the more frequently used, somewhat shopworn tunes particular to specific prayers. Cantor Goffin contrasts his approach with that of other cantors at that time:

> Most *chazzanim* at every major shul did *chazzanut* [cantorial pieces]. That's what they were expected to do, and they did very little singing. If they did congregational singing, he [the cantor] would start something and the congregation would do it.[5] He rarely sang. And

---

[5] The Young Israel movement, which had reached its peak around the time Lincoln Square began, was known for the congregational singing in its affiliated synagogues,

congregational singing was the old stuff, and things that were really stale. It was rare to hear contemporary *nigunim* [tunes]. It [doing contemporary tunes] was something I liked. Rabbi Riskin, you know, he wasn't the type of rabbi to sit back in a chair and listen to the *chazzan*. He sang with you, he got up, he banged on the table... He wanted a guy who could play guitar to become his chazzan, which, in those days was an anathema, because, first of all, a guitar player... in the early days of the folk genre, that was like rock-and-roll today. If you played guitar, you were a secularist, so no shul would even think of hiring a guy who played the guitar. But that's what he wanted; he wanted that type of thing.

At Lincoln Square Synagogue, congregants who were essentially newcomers to Judaism experienced prayer with joy and awe for the first time. The contrasting spiritual elements of elation and deep concentration that were an integral part of the prayer service at LSS were frequently missing in typical Orthodox synagogues, where Jews with a religious upbringing tended to be scornful and cynical in their attitude towards spiritual and heartfelt prayer.[6] The cynicism was born out of nervousness

which was a departure from the operatic cantor. However, most Young Israel synagogues did not have resident cantors, and they were certainly not as innovative as Sherwood Goffin in their choice of tunes for congregational singing. But the main difference is that the attendees of the Young Israels were, by and large, people from Orthodox backgrounds who knew the prayer service, with all of the plusses and minuses which that background implied.

6 Samuel C. Heilman has identified a synagogue phenomenon he calls "quasi-chazzanic activity," which is the audible praying on the part of some members of the congregation, which often cues the cantor as to when to finish one prayer and begin another (Heilman, *Synagogue Life*, 88–91). Not mentioned by Heilman is the fact that in addition to cuing the cantor (and broadcasting knowledge and/or piety, according to Heilman), this "hum" or "buzz" of prayer is a regular feature of Orthodox and other synagogues in which there are knowledgeable worshippers, and, even without audible cues to the cantor, gives the feeling that there is "prayer happening." In the early days of Lincoln Square, there was very little "quasi-chazzanic activity" because very few of the congregants knew how to pray or felt comfortable praying audibly. This made Sherwood Goffin's job doubly challenging,

regarding change in general, and the perception of prayer not as a way of communicating with God but as simply another Jewish ritual.

Rabbi Riskin's aim was to create a new experience in Modern Orthodox prayer, and, with the help of Sherwood Goffin, who was blessed with musical talent as well as a unique spiritual approach to prayer, the rabbi succeeded. The young rabbi had discovered a way of teaching faith that was different from lectures, classes, and sermons, yet worked in harmony with these educational tools, and he had found a partner in Cantor Sherwood Goffin, whose faith-driven singing would pervade Lincoln Square Synagogue for years to come.[7]

because he often had to provide his own "quasi-chazzanic activity" by praying audibly in between the points where the cantor traditionally chants. Cantor Goffin also overcame this problem by an increased amount of congregational singing, even in places where the cantor traditionally chants alone.

[7] Cantor Sherwood Goffin holds seniority at Lincoln Square Synagogue. Now in his forty-first year of service there, he still maintains the same high level of spirituality in his leadership of the prayers.

✎ 8 ✎

SHABBAT

CAN WE EVER REGAIN the glorious vision of Sabbath as a radiant
queen, a jeweled sovereign who comes to visit bringing warmth and
joy in her train? The poor and often inept Hasidic Jews in the stories
of Isaac Bashevis Singer may bicker and complain, and they surely
suffer, but when the sun goes down and the lamps begin to flicker on
Friday evening, a kind of magic touches their world. Special cakes
have been baked, and now the sacred candles are lighted. Sabbath is
an eternity in time, as Abraham Heschel says; it is a cathedral made
not with stones and glass but with hours and minutes. It is a sacred
symbol that no one can tear down or destroy. It comes every week,
inviting human beings not to strive and succeed, not even to pray very
much, but to taste and know that God is good, that the earth and the
flesh are there to be shared and enjoyed.

These words were written not by a rabbi or Jewish educator, but by Harvey
Cox, a Christian theologian and divinity professor at Harvard,[1] in his 1977
book, *Turning East: Why Americans Look to the Orient for Spirituality and What
That Search Can Mean to the West.*[2] Cox's poignant depiction of the beauty of
Shabbat could easily have been expressed by Rabbi Riskin in 1964, as he
began his work at Lincoln Square Synagogue.

---

[1] Harvey Cox gained fame and popularity after the publication of *The Secular City* in
1965. I have based a great deal of my research about the state of religion in the
1960s on this book.

[2] New York, Simon and Schuster, 1977, 70–71.

From the beginning of his career, Rabbi Riskin was committed to making Shabbat – not just the Shabbat services – the center of his congregants' life. He taught and preached about Shabbat more than any other area of Jewish life. Of course, it could be said that as the focal point of the Jewish week, Shabbat was the primary focus of Lincoln Square Synagogue (and virtually every other synagogue as well). If congregants observed Shabbat, they came to the synagogue on Shabbat. If large numbers of people came to synagogue on Shabbat, the synagogue, almost by definition, was successful.

Rabbi Riskin, however, had a far deeper reason for placing Shabbat at the center of his teaching and preaching. Shabbat was a testimony to God's existence and His creation of the world, and so this day of rest called for a rendezvous with God. The rabbi explains the depth of his emotions about the sanctity of Shabbat in the following way:

> I believed then as I believe now – that the quintessence of Judaism is Shabbat. The sanctity of Judaism is seen within Shabbat as the melding together of the spiritual and the physical, the intellectual and the emotional. Shabbat speaks to the soul and to the mind at the same time. There is no experience as rich as Shabbat in expressing the truth of Judaism and enabling people to grow.

But how do you teach the beauty and spirit of Shabbat to individuals who have never before experienced it and who are largely unaware of its significance?[3] It is true that the Shabbat services at Lincoln Square

---

[3] Because the reality is so different today, it is difficult to convey the lack of respect of the vast majority of American Jews in the 1960s for traditional Sabbath and Jewish holiday observance. My mother was fired from the Chemical Bank of New York in 1968 because she did not come to work on the first two days of the holiday of Sukkot. When she asked why she was being fired for observance of a religious holiday, they told her that they had taken a poll of the Jewish executives at Chemical, and the result of the poll was that Sukkot (the first two days of which, according to Jewish Law, are similar to Shabbat in their prohibitions of work) is a minor Jewish holiday. Anyone who has studied Judaism seriously knows the centrality of Sukkot as a major festival in the Jewish calendar; this was a classical

Synagogue were well attended, but they didn't take up more than five hours out of the twenty-five hours of Shabbat. Most of the real observance of Shabbat takes place in the Jewish home: Kiddush, the special meals, the singing of songs around the table, and, of course, the observance of the Shabbat laws.

Rabbi Riskin could have stood at the podium week after week and preached about the joy and fulfillment to be found in Shabbat observance, but that alone would not have been effective in demonstrating to his congregants the ultimate value of Shabbat. In Rabbi Riskin's mind, the best way to educate was not only through words, but through action and by example.[4]

Together with his wife Vicky, he opened up his home to his congregants and invited them to eat at his Shabbat table so that they could observe and experience the holiness of the day for themselves. Each week, he welcomed

---

case of ignorance on the part of Jewish people about their own heritage – leading to a lack of respect for Jewish observance and intolerance of a Jew who chose to observe.

[4] I recall one particular incident in 1970 in which Rabbi Riskin demonstrated to his synagogue that he was going to practice what he preached. It was Erev (the eve of) Yom Kippur and the Lincoln Square congregants had just finished reciting *Mincha* (the Afternoon Service, traditionally recited before the final meal preceding the fast). Rabbi Riskin explained to his congregants the law/custom of males immersing themselves in a *mikveh* (ritual bath) before Yom Kippur in order to purify themselves in anticipation of the holy day.

Following his explanation, the rabbi announced, "I'm going to the *mikveh* now. Please come with me, if you wish." Although many of our wives went to the *mikveh* on a regular basis, most of us had never observed this custom. Nevertheless, we decided to follow the rabbi, and marched behind him in a procession up Broadway to 78th Street where the *mikveh* was located, and "took the plunge."

I would venture to say that it was very unusual in those days for Modern Orthodox men to go to the *mikveh* on Erev Yom Kippur, and, if they did, they did so as individuals, not as part of a "congregational field trip." But Rabbi Riskin knew that we had not been exposed to this tradition through our families, so in his uninhibited way, he included it in the synagogue experience.

between five and ten guests per meal to his modest apartment in 150 West End Avenue, just above the original temporary facility of the synagogue. For most of these guests, the experience at the Riskin's Shabbat table was new, different, and even exotic. The meals were always filled with lively singing and incisive analysis of the words of Torah, and ended with the heartfelt singing of Grace after Meals. Even in this relaxed atmosphere, Rabbi Riskin was always "on," and would recount, with an exuberance that seemed energized by Shabbat itself, wonderful stories which celebrated Shabbat and its extra measure of spirituality. The guests left with an altered perception of Shabbat. They began to think that perhaps Shabbat was not just a day of restrictions and limitations, as they had always believed, but a time of deep enjoyment and pleasure.

As important as his Shabbat hospitality was, Rabbi Riskin understood that it wasn't sufficient to invite five or ten people to each Shabbat meal. He needed to reach a critical mass of people in the congregation in order to make Shabbat a real "factor" in the life of the Lincoln Square community. Rabbi Riskin turned to two outgoing and friendly women in his congregation for help.

Mrs. A[5] and Mrs. B, as Rabbi Riskin called them, would often invite guests to their own homes on Shabbat, and were therefore the perfect choice to be partners in helping the rabbi to expose people to Shabbat. Each week, Rabbi Riskin asked Mrs. A and Mrs. B to invite the guests that he could not accommodate in his home in addition to the guests they invited. Thus, the power of Shabbat was increased threefold and a critical mass was becoming more attainable.

---

[5] Mrs. A was my mother, Anne Abramson, of blessed memory. She was a very sociable woman with a deep desire to continually meet new people. Rabbi Riskin's "mission" to create Shabbat in the community enabled her to do just that and to be at the center of creative process. Mrs. B is Beatrice (Bess) Bergman, my mother's close friend and neighbor in Lincoln Towers. She, too, was extremely outgoing and hospitable. Together, the two women created a powerhouse of hospitality, enjoying themselves tremendously in the process. Rabbi Riskin says that he could not have created Shabbat in the community without them.

As more and more Lincoln Square congregants began to observe Shabbat, Rabbi Riskin made it known that according to Halacha, if a Jew observes Shabbat, he or she is also trusted on his or her observance of Kashrut, the dietary laws. He also reminded his congregants that keeping Shabbat properly included strict observance of the prohibitions against cooking food and the special manner of warming food on Shabbat. Therefore, explained the rabbi, if an individual was Shabbat-observant, Rabbi Riskin and his wife would gladly accept that person's invitation for a Shabbat meal. Workshop classes were held in the Adult Education Institute on Shabbat observance, and squads were established to *kasher* ("kosherize") kitchens for those who wished.[6] This act carried with it the pleasing message to the congregation that the rabbi and Vicky really wanted to socialize with members of the community on Shabbat as long as no Halachic barrier existed for them to do so. As can be imagined, it also served as an impetus for Rabbi Riskin's fans who were sitting on the fence about Shabbat observance to make the decision to increase their commitment. After a while, at Lincoln Square it became "in" to be Shabbat observant.

Looking back, it seems almost inconceivable that so many LSS congregants took the enormous step of deciding to observe Shabbat and keep kosher, which resulted in such dramatic changes to their lifestyles. The Lincoln Square worshippers may have found the experience of Shabbat to be spiritually enriching, but to actually observe all of the laws involved tremendous sacrifices. These Manhattan Jews had to relinquish many of their leisurely weekend activities, which, according to Jewish law, were prohibited on Shabbat. As for keeping kosher, a person had to rethink one of the most reflexive human activities – eating. What possessed the Lincoln Square congregants to take these two major leaps?

---

[6] The rabbi also made it clear to those who lived on higher floors in apartment buildings that according to the laws of Shabbat, one was not supposed to press the button for the elevator. While there are varying Halachic opinions, he tended to be lenient with these individuals and allowed them, with certain provisos, to allow the non-Jewish doorman to operate the elevator.

A large part of the answer lies in the notion of community. As William Zeckendorf and Robert Moses had noted, the urban landscape is a rough one and desperately needs softening if the human spirit is to soar in the way that it longs to do. The pleasant anonymity that a metropolis affords is a double-edged sword; a person who becomes anonymous is isolated from the community. Rabbi Riskin translated Zeckendorf's and Moses's longing for a softer cityscape into deeply religious terms. Rabbi Riskin taught passionately and persuasively that Judaism insisted upon community. "A Jew," he used to say, "cannot be a hermit," and he substantiated his statement by detailing the Jewish rituals which can only be performed in groups, as well as acts of charity and outreach which are rooted in communal relationships.

Rabbi Riskin preached that two things solidify a Jewish community: the sharing of food and the sharing of Shabbat. Food is at the center of the community, and Shabbat is at the center of the Jews' covenant with God. So convincingly did Rabbi Riskin place these ideas as cornerstones of the Jewish people's very existence that member after member of the congregation opted to participate in these two great communal foundations – keeping kosher and observing Shabbat.

Rabbi Riskin's willingness to accept an invitation for a Shabbat meal if one met the ritual requirements was never seen as patronizing; it was rather perceived as an expression of his perennial friendliness: It was as if he was conveying the message: "I'm eager to come to your home on Shabbat as long as we can partake together in these two communal cornerstones: Shabbat observance and eating kosher."

In 1980, a program called "A Taste of Shabbat" was introduced at Lincoln Square Synagogue. Jesse Cogan, an early LSS member, later conceived a new name for the program: "Turn Friday Night into Shabbos." The purpose of the highly-subsidized program was to offer a bi-annual communal Shabbat meal to unaffiliated Jews. Tickets to the first meal, which took place on June 6, 1980, were sold out weeks in advance, and four hundred people squeezed into the ballroom of LSS. Throughout the years, the program brought several hundred unaffiliated Jews into Lincoln Square Synagogue.

Although no statistics are available to quantify what proportion of Lincoln Square Synagogue's membership became Shabbat observant, at some point the pervasive effect of Shabbat observance became palpable in the community, creating an even deeper sense of shared experience and shared spirituality. Congregants could now invite each other for Shabbat meals with ease and regularity, and this, of course, increased the level of social interaction exponentially, leading to new relationships among the congregants.[7]

"Can we ever regain the glorious vision of Sabbath as a radiant queen?" Harvey Cox asked. That vision was not only regained, but actually nurtured and reworked, not in the sentimental setting of an Isaac Bashevis Singer story,[8] as Professor Cox would have it, but in a most unlikely setting: the very urban, very sophisticated Upper West Side of Manhattan.

Despite the study of the laws of Shabbat taking place in every yeshiva around the country, including Modern Orthodoxy's bastion, Yeshiva University, and despite majestic statements and stories in Jewish literature lauding Shabbat for its testimony to an inextricable bond between God and the Jewish people, Shabbat observance signified a burden rather than joy to the majority of American Jews in the 1960s. Rabbi Riskin's immense

---

[7] It is difficult to demonstrate this empirically, but I believe that the social nature of Shabbat, which for many years has characterized the Upper West Side and many other communities, began at Lincoln Square with the phenomenon described above. My strong impression is that prior to this time, Shabbat-observant families did, of course, extend invitations to those who did not experience Shabbat in their own homes, but from anecdotal evidence, it seems that families inviting families and, certainly, singles inviting singles for Shabbat only began in earnest at Lincoln Square.

[8] Isaac Bashevis Singer, who lived on the West Side, was once a guest at Rabbi Riskin's Shabbat table. Rabbi Riskin recalls that Singer expressed cynicism regarding the laws of Shabbat, in particular the law that forbids the use of electricity on Shabbat ("An Orthodox Jew will not push a button which takes no effort, but will walk up many floors, which takes a great effort"). As warm a picture as Singer evoked of Shabbat in the shtetl, he was clearly unaware that Shabbat could thrive in America, and could strike the Jewish soul just as deeply as it did in Europe.

accomplishment was that he removed the negative connotations that his congregants associated with Shabbat and demonstrated that Shabbat in its traditional observance was a day to be cherished and enjoyed. In time, the message went out and became part of the fabric of Jewish assumption, absorbed by rabbis and teachers to come, who did not know its source. The message was that modern, educated Jewish Americans, if taught and inspired, will want to observe Shabbat and will relish and savor the taste of the World to Come that it bestows upon them.

❧ 9 ❧

WOMEN AND JUDAISM

The Role of Women in Jewish Thought and Practice

THE DECADE OF THE 1960S witnessed a revival of the feminist movement, which was heralded by Betty Friedan's founding of the National Organization for Women (NOW) in 1966. The organization was born partly out of a growing frustration among women that as mothers and housewives, they had no identity of their own or independent role within society at large.

Within the Jewish community, the reemergence of feminism in the 1960s had a profound effect on the religious outlook of many Jewish women, who began to reevaluate and question their status in Judaism, particularly Orthodox Judaism, in which men seemed to play a dominant role. Why, for example, were women not accorded the honor of an *aliyah,* being called up to the public reading from the Torah scroll?[1] And why could women not lead the prayer services on weekdays as men did, or on Shabbat, when the cantor was not present? These questions, though not new or previously unarticulated, took on a greater immediacy in light of the burgeoning feminist movement.

From the beginning of his rabbinate, Rabbi Riskin emphasized the absolute equality of the sexes before God and never even remotely implied in any of his statements or sermons that he believed in the superiority of men over women. He repeatedly quoted Genesis 1:27, which speaks about

---

[1] This privilege involved the recitation of blessings thanking God for bestowing the wisdom of the Torah upon the Jewish people.

the human being as having been created in God's image, and then makes clear, "... male and female He created them." The rabbi insisted that any discussion of women in Judaism begin with that text and that premise.

Though the women of LSS appreciated Rabbi Riskin's interpretation of the Biblical text, they pressed the rabbi to elaborate and expand upon the theoretical ideal and to apply it to day-to-day Orthodox Jewish life.

Rabbi Riskin stated with clarity and confidence that the roles of men and women could be equal in worth, but different in practice. Jewish tradition placed the overall responsibility for the spiritual development of the home upon women. The rabbi emphasized the extreme importance of the Jewish home as the center for so many of the commandments, including the dietary laws, the laws of family purity (those rules which govern the sexual separation of a married couple every month and their rejoining), and the education of the children. Judaism and its traditions could not survive without a strong foundation, which was built during childhood in every Jewish home. Of course, Rabbi Riskin explained, a husband could share the responsibilities of the home with his wife – and the wife could become involved in synagogue and public religious life – but according to Jewish tradition, a woman's ultimate responsibility was her family and her home.

While this approach resonated with some of the female LSS members, not everyone felt satisfied by Rabbi Riskin's answers. Many of the Lincoln Square congregants had read Betty Friedan's *The Feminine Mystique* – the "bible" of the feminist movement – which attacked the popular notion that women could only find fulfillment through childbearing and homemaking. As a result of reading this book, LSS congregants – the women, in particular – had developed a greater consciousness about their role in life and in Judaism. On the subject of traditional Judaism and its attitudes towards women, Ms. Friedan wrote:

> Women of Orthodox Catholic or Jewish origin do not easily break through the housewife image; *it is enshrined in the canons of their religion* [emphasis mine], in the assumptions of their own and their husbands'

childhood, and in their church's dogmatic definitions of marriage and motherhood.[2]

Vicky Riskin recalls that the majority of the women in her classes for brides-to-be, in which the laws and the ethos of Jewish family life were studied and discussed, had read *The Feminine Mystique*. Vicky herself had read it and tried to be as sensitive as possible to the burgeoning feminist leanings of many of her students. Both Vicky and Rabbi Riskin faced a formidable challenge in helping modern women of the 1960s and 1970s understand the beauty of the traditional role of the Jewish woman.

Freda Birnbaum, a Jewish feminist and early Lincoln Square member, who described herself in those days as "Rabbi Riskin's pet gadfly," recalls:

> I [sometimes] had a feeling he [Rabbi Riskin] was being too apologetic for the party line. As things continued, I could see that he would respond to what he thought was a real need and not just a rant. And he would go to bat for these things even when there was opposition to them in some quarters [in the synagogue]. I know that some women were really annoyed with him because they thought he wasn't progressive enough about some of this, but it cannot be taken away from him that when he allowed something, he would stand behind it....

On the other hand, there were many men (as well as some women) who felt that Rabbi Riskin went overboard in accommodating the women in his synagogue. What was truly amazing was that the debate about women's role in Judaism, which had the potential to cause friction and polarization in the Modern Orthodox community, did not discourage women from attending and being active in Lincoln Square classes, prayers, and activities. Rabbi Riskin's congregants, his female ones in particular, realized that the rabbi was taking women's issues seriously and appreciated his ability to speak to all the variant viewpoints within the synagogue.[3]

---

[2] Betty Friedan, *The Feminine Mystique,* New York: W.W. Norton & Co, 1963, 351.

[3] It is noteworthy that much more recently, Rabbi Riskin has come out against the fairly new phenomenon of services which call themselves Orthodox in which

Probably more important than Rabbi Riskin's views and policies on women's participation in the synagogue was his ongoing emphasis of the importance of learning about the female figures in the Torah, their heroic actions, and their intrinsic worth. This was crucial because as feminism developed in American society in the 1960s and 1970s, there were many accusations leveled against certain distinctive features of traditional Judaism that seemed, on the surface at least, to be anti-woman. One such criticism made mention of the daily blessing recited by Jewish men thanking God "for not having made me a woman," and also referenced the Talmudic dictum that "women are of light minds."

Unlike many Orthodox rabbis, Rabbi Riskin had no trouble admitting that the rabbis of the Talmud lived and worked in their own era and, although their greatness generally enabled them to see beyond themselves and their age, they had their own biases. But Rabbi Riskin insisted that these statements be seen in their context and taught many other rabbinical texts that demonstrated the rabbis' nuanced respect for women and a deep understanding of feminine spirituality. To be sure, these classical Jewish texts did not usually solve contemporary feminist conundrums such as expanding women's role in the synagogue and other rituals. As a result, female congregants often claimed that the rabbi, in his explanation of the sources, was engaging in apologetics. But Rabbi Riskin's desire to listen attentively to incipient feminist voices and his attempt to reconcile classic Jewish attitudes with modern philosophies was, in fact, revolutionary.

---

women lead some of the non-minyan-requiring prayers, and, most especially, read the Torah and receive *aliyot*. The rabbi rejects these practices on the grounds that they conflict with *Halacha*. He still believes that women should be permitted to be involved in prayer and Torah to the greatest extent the *Halacha* allows, but not beyond that. As always, he has taken a difficult stance; it is always easier to be a complete rejectionist or an extreme inclusionist. But the reasoned middle path continues to be his hallmark.

The Role of Women in the Synagogue: The Mechitza

The installation of a *mechitza*, a partition separating men from women in the synagogue, was a contentious issue when Rabbi Riskin assumed the pulpit at Lincoln Square. The popular opinion among Reform and Conservative Jews was that the *mechitza* was anti-feminist in nature, and that its purpose was to prevent women from active involvement in the prayer service. Rabbi Riskin went to great pains – both in the original converted apartment in Lincoln Towers and later in the new building on Amsterdam Avenue – to counter the notion that the *mechitza* was intended to exclude women. In the original apartment, he decreed that the *mechitza* divide the room down the middle so that both men and women would be able to observe what was taking place. Such a division was uncommon in most Orthodox synagogues, where the women were often relegated to the rear of the synagogue or to a high balcony.

Chaya Gorsetman, an early LSS congregant, grew up in a traditional Orthodox synagogue with a balcony for women, but became increasingly interested in feminism throughout her adult life.

> I'm not sitting on top in the yoo-hoo place anymore. That was a major issue for me. Not from a feminist point of view, but from an inclusionary point of view. [I feel that] I'm part of it now. It was uncomfortable at first, but I loved it. I said, "I'm sitting here. I am part of this service." A feminist today would think I was nuts, but it's all where you come from.

In the new synagogue on Amsterdam Avenue, the *mechitza* that was built was even more revolutionary. The synagogue seating was arranged in a semi-circle with the rows of seats rising progressively like seats in a theater. The women's and men's sections were placed adjacent to one another with a rather inconspicuous partition dividing them.[4] Rabbi Riskin constructed this

---

[4] Although the *mechitza* was revolutionary in its inconspicuousness, Rabbi Riskin ensured that it conformed to halachic guidelines.

design in order to demonstrate that the purpose of a *mechitza* in an Orthodox synagogue is not to demean women.

An Equal Voice for Men and Women

As an Orthodox rabbi, Rabbi Riskin was acutely aware of the traditional halachic viewpoint regarding women's involvement in the prayer service. Although he knew that he could not permit women to be called to the Torah or to lead the prayer services, he did make sure to involve them as much as was permissible according to Jewish law.

At one point, the rabbi instituted a "question period" following the reading of the Torah on Shabbat morning. He felt that it was important that the worshippers should be given the opportunity to ask questions and to express their thoughts. Congregants would raise their hands and ask any questions they had, whether on the content of that week's Torah reading or on another Jewish topic that was of interest to them. The questions – about four were taken per session – were not pre-screened, and Rabbi Riskin tried to give as full an answer as he could within a reasonable time limit.[5]

The rabbi insisted upon taking an approximately equal number of questions from women as from men. This seemingly minor innovation was met with criticism from some of the more traditional members, who were unaccustomed to hearing the sound of women's voices from the women's section of the sanctuary. Rabbi Riskin, however, fiercely defended his practice, and it remained in force. While this victory may seem insignificant by today's standards, it demonstrated that Rabbi Riskin was determined to grant his female congregants equality when it did not conflict with Halacha.

---

[5] The practice was eventually discontinued as a result of the consensus that it protracted an already rather lengthy service, making prolonged concentration on the prayers difficult.

Women's Participation on Sukkot

In 1972, Rabbi Riskin responded to what he perceived as a sincere feminist cause in an even more radical way: He permitted a group of women to hold a private prayer service on Simchat Torah, the holiday in which the annual cycle of the Torah reading is completed and begun anew. The female participants were able to dance and rejoice in the *bet midrash* with the Torah scrolls, but would not recite any parts of the service that required a halachic *minyan,* or quorum of ten men.[6] Afterwards, Rabbi Riskin spoke emotionally and eloquently about the testimonials of women who explained to him what it meant to them to finally hold and embrace a Torah scroll. Although he received criticism from many of his more traditional members for permitting this service to take place,[7] he felt that he was on solid ground halachically and could not imagine depriving women of this experience.

Rabbi Riskin faced yet another challenge shortly after the move to the new synagogue building in 1971. It was the holiday of Sukkot, in which Jews are commanded to eat their meals in a temporary structure called the *sukka*. Lincoln Square Synagogue constructed a large *sukka* adjacent to the building and catering was arranged for the first two evening meals of the holiday. As was the case with virtually every activity taking place within the synagogue, virtually all of the congregants wanted to participate. Soon the meals were over-booked, and there was simply no more room in the *sukka*. One of the more traditional members came up with a solution: Since, technically, only males are commanded by the Torah to eat in the *sukka,* the caterer should

---

[6] Ordinarily, in Orthodox synagogues, the dancing with the Torah scrolls takes place in the men's section of the synagogue while the women observe the festivities from their section.

[7] The criticism was not limited only to LSS members. It came from many quarters, and it was sharp. One prominent West Side rabbi of the time told Rabbi Riskin that his synagogue could no longer be considered Orthodox, even though Rabbi Riskin says he consulted with Rabbi Soloveitchik, Rabbi Moshe Feinstein and the Lubavitcher Rebbe on the matter.

set up the meals for the men inside the *sukka,* and the women would be accommodated in the adjacent social hall.

From a technical Jewish legal perspective, it was a good solution, but Rabbi Riskin would not hear of it. Invoking the Talmud's dictum of *teshvu ke-eyn taduru,* that one should live in the *sukka* during the holiday as one lives in one's home during the rest of the year, the rabbi insisted that members should be accommodated as families – men and women together – according to the order of their registration for the event.

Rabbi Riskin was not operating in a vacuum at Lincoln Square when he dealt with matters that related to women. There was a core of knowledgeable, observant congregants who were, in a way, the synagogue's "bread and butter." They were the men who made up the daily *minyan,* attended the rabbi's Shabbat Talmud class regularly, and asked intelligent and informed questions. However, most of these European-bred men were far more committed to traditional Jewish practice than they were to understanding feminist trends in American society. So when Rabbi Riskin had to make decisions regarding women's participation in LSS life, he not only had to ensure that the practice was consonant with Halacha, but he also had to be sensitive to whether his nucleus of observant regulars would be able to accept a practice that they had never before witnessed in their previous synagogue experiences.

For the most part, Rabbi Riskin managed to avoid alienating his core group. These members – the only ones who were really concerned about strict conformation with Halacha – loved Rabbi Riskin dearly and, although his interpretations sometimes differed from what they were used to, they trusted him as a rabbi who was fiercely loyal to the Orthodox tradition.

The Orthodox Bat Mitzvah

Orthodox Halachic authorities had been deeply troubled by the development of the Bat Mitzvah ceremony, which they felt characterized the divergent Conservative and Reform movements. While all rabbinic scholars agreed that a young girl at age twelve becomes legally responsible to perform the

Torah commandments, most Orthodox *poskim* (rabbinic scholars who make Jewish legal decisions) felt that it was inappropriate to mark the occasion with a public ceremony in light of the fact that adult women did not publicly participate in the synagogue service. All attempts at creating various types of pseudo-services in which the bat mitzvah girl could take a leadership role were frowned upon.

Rabbi Riskin also felt that creating a one-time bogus service for the occasion – as was done by some Orthodox congregations – was meaningless both to the bat mitzvah girl and to the congregation. What would be the point in arranging a special prayer service for the bat mitzvah girl if she would never be able to replicate the experience again within the walls of the synagogue? However, he did feel strongly that a bat mitzvah ceremony was crucial for young women to mark their coming of age to perform *mitzvot*. Therefore, he instituted a bat mitzvah ceremony at LSS. These events were usually held on Friday evenings either in place of the regular Oneg Shabbat or, in later years after the cessation of the Oneg Shabbat, as a specially scheduled ceremony. Sometimes the bat mitzvah girl's family chose to conduct the ceremony on a Sunday or on an evening during the week so that they could play music at the reception, which would not be possible on Shabbat due to Shabbat restrictions. The young woman would give a serious *devar Torah*, a scholarly speech that she wrote, usually based upon the Torah portion of the week or on a particular topic that interested her. Rabbi Riskin acted as the consultant to the bat mitzvah celebrant and would guide her in the preparatory study and construction of the speech.

After the bat mitzvah girl's speech, Rabbi Riskin would then deliver his own speech. He always emphasized at these bat mitzvah celebrations how important it was that young Jewish women learn to study and teach Torah on the same level as men. While Rabbi Riskin marshaled Halachic sources to support that argument, the strength and conviction of his opinions in this matter were surely a result of his childhood Torah study sessions with his cherished, beloved grandmother.

Although the description of the bat mitzvah ceremony now seems rather prosaic, what is important to note is that Rabbi Riskin was not attempting to mimic the bar mitzvah ceremony. Rather, he was intent on creating a unique experience for the bat mitzvah girls in which they would have the opportunity to show their interest and proficiency in studying and transmitting Torah. The message was clear: women were just as capable of learning Torah as men, and as they marked their coming of age with their bat mitzvah ceremony, they were encouraged to do so.

ॐ ॐ

Thanks to the revival of feminism, Jewish women in the 1960s were beginning to find their voice, but in most traditional Orthodox synagogues at the time, that voice was not taken seriously. Instead of welcoming the opportunity to find ways to support and accommodate their female congregants, most Orthodox rabbis chose to ignore their needs. Acknowledging the women's cause would require a reexamination of the Jewish laws concerning women, and that was simply not an option. Instead, they preferred to avoid any potentially inflammatory issues, hoping that any dissenting voices would disappear.

Rabbi Riskin was not weighed down by the same fears and insecurities that plagued other Orthodox rabbis of his day. It was abundantly clear to his congregants that he was as comfortable talking to women as he was men, and as a result, he was approachable. In addition, since he was a brilliant Torah scholar, he was not nervous about making changes when they were permissible within the boundaries of the Halacha.

The creation of a new Orthodox synagogue in the midst of a feminist revolution could potentially have been disastrous, resulting in further disillusionment among women in Orthodox Judaism. The *mechitza*, with its seemingly exclusionary walls, created a feeling of disconnection among women. Even certain prayers appeared to be demeaning. How could women possibly feel equal before God with such barriers? Rabbi Riskin ensured the congregation's ultimate success by allowing his female congregants to find their own distinct voice and place within the parameters of Orthodox Judaism.

REACHING OUT

WHAT HAPPENED WITHIN the four walls of Lincoln Square Synagogue was truly miraculous. Thousands of people were empowered to reclaim their Jewish heritage through intense and productive study. Lincoln Square became a community that not only recognized Shabbat but longed for its weekly arrival, observing it with joy and vitality. Holidays were seen as a rendezvous with God, reliving the Exodus from Egypt, the Revelation at Sinai, and the divine protection in the desert.

One might have thought that after all of Rabbi Riskin's monumental accomplishments within the synagogue, a comfortable plateau had been reached and all future efforts would be directed towards maintaining the strong sense of community that had been created. However, maintenance was not in Rabbi Riskin's temperament. He was convinced that Torah was for all Jews, not just for those who had chosen to be involved with Lincoln Square Synagogue. It occurred to Rabbi Riskin to wonder: if so many people were coming in off the street in order to attend the LSS services and lectures, how many more Jews must there be who had never set foot inside the synagogue, either because they did not know of its existence or because they had no motivation to be there? That being the case, the Rabbi asked himself, why should the synagogue not come to them?[1]

---

[1] In order to understand why, up until this point, there had been so few attempts at synagogue outreach, we must take note of the fact that in order to be successful, there always needs to be an individual who believes in the goal and the process with every fiber of his being. As discussed in Chapter 3, "The Teacher," this was the case

The notion of reaching out to Jews beyond one's immediate environment was uncommon in the 1960s and 1970s. There was no movement afoot at that time to approach an unaffiliated Jew with the purpose of revitalizing his or her Judaism.[2] True, if a rabbi of a particular community or a campus Hillel could find ways of encouraging his congregants or students to become involved in Jewish activities, that was fine – he was, after all, engaged by the community or by the Hillel chapter to do just that. But to actually go beyond the bounds of community out to the street, to find Jews who had no interest in Judaism and somehow get them to engage their Jewish identity was unheard of. For most people, reaching

---

with Dr. Abraham Stern and Torah Leadership Seminar when it came to reaching out to non-observant high-school youth, with Rabbi Morris Besdin and the James Striar School regarding college-age students, and with Rabbi Riskin concerning adults.

Perhaps Rabbi Riskin was faced with the greatest challenge of all because the prevailing assumption was that high-school and college students are still malleable, whereas adults are set in their ways and are less amenable to making major life changes. Nevertheless, Rabbi Riskin proved that if the vision is clear enough and the will is strong enough, there are no barriers to success.

[2] It is true that since Rabbi Menachem Mendel Schneerson became the rebbe in 1950, Chabad Lubavitch came up with the idea of spreading Jewish observance beyond the already-committed religious community. But in those early years, Chabad directed much of its energy towards aiding Jews in Europe, primarily the Soviet Union, whose observance of Judaism and often their very lives were under constant threat by the authorities. To that end, Lubavitch would send emissaries – a concept which would later be modified and extended to the United States and the rest of the Free World – to Russia to teach and support these oppressed Jews.

New Yorkers of the 1960s also recall Chabad Jews walking through the streets of Brooklyn offering unaffiliated Jews the *lulav* and *etrog* (special plants for the Sukkot holiday) and visiting various synagogues in order to enhance the dancing on Simchat Torah (the joyous culmination of that holiday). However, only in the mid-1970s did Chabad's outreach become organized on a large scale. Interestingly, the first "Mitzvah Tank," Chabad's traveling outreach vehicle, first appeared on the streets of New York in 1974. The Lincoln Square Torah Van began its travels in 1973.

out beyond one's community of Jews to other Jews was equivalent to proselytizing. Virtually no one thought to put into practice the idea of helping one's fellow Jew encounter the Jewish tradition although that concept was found in many classical Jewish texts.

Rabbi Riskin's vision of moving out of the synagogue to encounter Jews on the street shattered the popular notion that Jewish spiritual leadership required the rabbi to try to encourage people to *come into* the synagogue.[3] Once Rabbi Riskin conceived of the "total outreach" concept, it became clear that he would need assistance in carrying it out. Since he was heavily involved with everything that was taking place within the synagogue, it would be impossible for him to devote the time necessary to spearhead the actual movement outside of the synagogue. The rabbi turned to Ephraim Z. Buchwald, whom he had hired in 1972 to teach at the Joseph Shapiro Academy.

Prior to teaching at the JSA, Ephraim Buchwald had taught at the Ramaz School, a Modern Orthodox Jewish day school in Manhattan known for its academic excellence. Rabbi Riskin first encountered Ephraim at Camp Yaron, a camp for Americans located in Israel, where Ephraim worked as a counselor. Since Rabbi Riskin had been spending his summers in Israel in the early 1970s, he had a chance to observe Ephraim Buchwald in action. Deeply impressed by Ephraim's warm and friendly personality as well as by his ability to communicate easily with the campers, Rabbi Riskin asked him to become a teacher at the Joseph Shapiro Academy while he was completing his studies for rabbinic ordination at Yeshiva University.

---

[3] As mentioned previously, Lincoln Square's "street outreach" shortly preceded Lubavitch's appearance on the streets of New York. More important than the chronology, though, is the major difference in goals. Lubavitch's goal was always the performance of the *mitzvot* in the Mitzvah Tanks – putting on *tefillin*, sitting in a *sukka*, reciting a blessing. While Rabbi Riskin valued any *mitzvah* performed "on the street," he saw Lincoln Square's movement to the street as a function of community. His aim was to inspire residents of the Lincoln Square neighborhood to attend the various religious and educational functions of Lincoln Square Synagogue and become a part of the Lincoln Square Synagogue community.

Left to right: Rabbi Riskin, Cantor Goffin (with son Eli), and Rabbi Buchwald, 1977. Credit: Riskin family photo.

Lincoln Square Synagogue model seder on Broadway and 72nd St., circa 1973.
At microphone, Cantor Sherwood Goffin.
Leading seder: Rabbi Ephraim Buchwald. Credit: LSS archives.

Ephraim accepted the position and during his first year at LSS, he proved to be both an excellent educator and organizer. Rabbi Riskin decided to put Ephraim Buchwald in charge of the JSA.

The Academy had become a major player in adult Jewish education in New York, with hundreds of students enrolled in its classes. After having taught at Ramaz, Rabbi Buchwald felt confident in his abilities in the area of education, but outreach was a new concept that required a great deal of thought.

The Lincoln Square Torah Van

The question of how to do Jewish outreach occupied Rabbi Buchwald's thoughts day and night. One day, he found inspiration in a newspaper article that reported that New York's Jacobi Hospital had sent its personnel traveling around the city in a van, dispensing medical advice and social services to people who would not or could not come to the hospital. It occurred to Rabbi Buchwald that a similar idea could be employed in the new field of Jewish outreach.

Rabbi Buchwald immediately brought the idea to Rabbi Riskin, who had just received a substantial donation from the family of Joseph Shapiro, for whom the Academy was named. Rabbi Riskin listened to the idea with great interest. He recalled having seen Lubavitch – later to become famous for their "street" outreach – driving through the streets of Manhattan with a mobile *sukka* (the hut used for that autumn holiday). Rabbi Riskin decided to use a substantial part of the donation for the purchase of a brand-new 24-foot Winnebago, which, after its kitchen was removed and a Torah Ark installed, was dubbed the Lincoln Square Torah Van.

The LSS Torah Van was "an incredible marketing device," but in a sense it was more than that. It was a symbol of the synagogue's desire to meet Jewish people where they were and educate them – not by demanding anything from them, but by giving to them. The van, which was usually parked near the extremely busy intersection of 72nd Street and Broadway, just a few blocks from the synagogue, contained members of the LSS educational staff and some volunteers. They would approach individuals whom they thought were Jewish and would hand them symbols of the upcoming holiday: honey for Rosh Hashana, used as a symbol for a sweet New Year; candles for Chanukah and flowers that traditionally adorn the home and the synagogue for the late spring holiday of Shavuot. On the Sunday before Passover, Rabbi Buchwald and Cantor Goffin would lead a model Seder – the special Passover meal – at the corner of 72nd and Broadway. During Chanukah, Lincoln Square erected a giant Menorah on that same corner and held nightly celebrations with candle-lighting and the distribution of candles, menorahs, latkes, and jelly doughnuts to passersby.

On Purim, Rabbi Buchwald and his staff distributed hundreds of *mishloach manot* (food gifts for the Purim holiday) on the street. On December 25th, during the public school Christmas vacation, the synagogue hosted "Feel Jewish" parties for elementary school students. Cantor Goffin would also hold *kumzitzes* (Jewish song sessions) in the Lincoln Towers buildings to attract residents to the synagogue. Of course, accompanying all of these activities were brochures describing the synagogue's activities, particularly the adult education classes. The public was startled; rarely were gifts given on the street without a catch. But here the only catch was a low-key invitation to join the Lincoln Square Synagogue community.

During the summer of 1973, a group of volunteers attempted to help the Lincoln Square approach to outreach "go national." The group made arrangements with several Jewish communities, mostly in the South and Midwest, to park the Torah Van in each of their communities for two or three days and "do their thing" for members of the local Jewish community. The experiment was a resounding success, and leaders of the communities in question thanked Lincoln Square profusely for their efforts and for bringing the warmth of outreach to their cities.

The Beginners Service

It is hard to imagine that there was ever a clearer demonstration of Jewish educators and rabbis going outside the synagogue and educating and inspiring Jews on the streets. Needless to say, these activities attracted hundreds of Jewish people from the neighborhood to Lincoln Square Synagogue. But the success of the outreach activities – and of Rabbi Riskin's growing reputation – produced a problem which was prosaic, yet increasingly serious: overcrowding.

Hundreds of people flocked to Lincoln Square's main sanctuary to attend Rabbi Riskin's Wednesday evening lectures, and the 480 seats were quickly filled. But hundreds more students would arrive shortly after, only to discover that there were no empty seats to be found. Many often ended up standing in the aisles and the stairways. The problem was ameliorated – if not solved – by directing the overflow of attendees to the large ballroom downstairs, where they could listen to the lecture broadcast electronically.

The issue of overcrowding was most apparent during the Shabbat morning services, when the sanctuary attracted more people than it could hold, creating unsafe and uncomfortable conditions once again. As well as the logistical problems caused by the overcrowding, an atmosphere of tension pervaded the synagogue when synagogue members arrived on Shabbat morning to find that their seats had been taken by outside members of the public who had either heard about Rabbi Riskin through the grapevine or attended classes during the week but had no formal connection with the synagogue.

The topic of overcrowding was discussed at every Board of Trustees meeting, and it was during one of those meetings that Rabbi Riskin hit upon a solution. In 1974, he asked Rabbi Buchwald, in whom he had placed so much trust to run the educational program, to conduct an "overflow" service on Shabbat morning that would run parallel to the regular service led by Rabbi Riskin and Cantor Goffin. Rabbi Buchwald's initial reaction to Rabbi Riskin's idea was negative. What was the point of creating a parallel service to the most popular Orthodox service in New York? Jews were turning up in droves to Lincoln Square Synagogue specifically because of Rabbi Riskin and Cantor Sherwood Goffin. If this winning combination were to be removed from the formula, what appeal would the "overflow" service have to worshippers? Moreover, how would they be able to decide which people would be directed to the "overflow" service – would it be only for latecomers once all the seats had been filled? What would be the nature of the service?

In the end, Rabbi Buchwald agreed to lead a parallel service on Shabbat morning at Lincoln Square Synagogue, but it was not the type of service that Rabbi Riskin had in mind, nor was it created for the purpose of solving the problem of overcrowding.[4]

The real impetus for this service appeared in the form of Steve Reich, a 38-year-old composer of music who, back in the early seventies, was just becoming popular.[5] Steve and his then-girlfriend, now wife, Meryl Korot, began to attend Rabbi Buchwald's weekly Bible class in the Joseph Shapiro Academy. Both conscientious students, Steve and Meryl were fascinated by Rabbi Buchwald's profound presentation of the biblical narrative. Gradually the couple increased their level of Jewish observance and chose to become more involved in synagogue life. However, there was one problem that needed to be overcome – the prayer service, which was lengthy and in Hebrew, was just too difficult for them. Steve and Meryl, who became close to Rabbi Buchwald, asked him to form a special service on Shabbat for beginners. Steve Reich reflected later, "There were no courses on how to pray, and it was sort of odd to ask for one,"[6] but Rabbi Buchwald, intrigued with the idea, agreed to go ahead with the beginners' service.

Interestingly, the idea did not take off immediately. The Lincoln Square Synagogue Beginners Service began in the fall of 1975 and was held in Classroom 1, a small, unassuming room on the second floor of the synagogue that had the capacity to hold fifty people. For six months, the

---

[4] That "overflow" service was ultimately undertaken by Rabbi Cohen and has become a fixture in the synagogue over the years. It is now known as the Rabbi Herschel Cohen Memorial Minyan.

[5] Steve Reich is now heralded as one of America's greatest living composers, the father of the minimalist movement in music. He is an observant Jew who has used Jewish themes in his music.

[6] Kenneth A. Briggs, "Synagogue Acts to Help Jews to Renew Their Faith." *New York Times*, March 28, 1981.

group consisted of just Rabbi Buchwald, Steve and Meryl, and a young, tall accountant who, coincidentally, was also named Stephen Reich.[7] Rabbi Buchwald points out how unlikely it seemed at the time that anyone would choose to attend a service with a "belittling" name like the Beginners Service rather than go to the "best show in town," the service with Rabbi Riskin and Cantor Goffin.

But little by little, participants started to turn up for the Beginners service, and they wasted no time in spreading the word to others how this service helped them understand the structure of the service, the content of the prayers, the idea of prayer itself, and the message of Shabbat, as explained by Rabbi Buchwald.

Rabbi Buchwald notes:

> Some "regulars" from the main sanctuary began to attend the service to learn the basics of Hebrew prayer that they had never mastered, and then returned to the main sanctuary.

It is important to note that the Beginners Service did not contain all of the traditional elements of a service. Although there was a *mechitza* in place and the Torah portion of the week was discussed, the full service was not recited and there was no actual Torah reading. As has already been discussed, Rabbi Riskin created and ran a similar type of service late Friday evening as a concession to the original Conservative-leaning founders. Friday night was one thing, but to create an abridged service on Shabbat morning – the main prayer service of Shabbat – was a bold step. But, amazingly, because of the atmosphere that prevailed at Lincoln Square, the participants in the Beginners Service were not only tolerated, but lionized as the real heroes of the synagogue – individuals who recognized their lack of Jewish background and set out to do something about it.

---

[7] Like so much that happened at Lincoln Square, there were moments of comic relief. Rabbi Buchwald recalls that, in addition to the three participants and himself, every second week, "One strange character would come in on roller skates, tennis racket in hand, and ask: 'How do you know that there is a God?'"

The tipping point came on Shabbat, March 28, 1981, when the *New York Times* ran a story on the front page of its second section (which often featured stories about trend-setting events or institutions) about the Beginners Service, with the headline, "Synagogue Acts to Help Jews to Renew Their Faith." The article featured the stories of some of the Beginners Service participants, including Steve Reich, whom they dubbed "the avant-garde composer," and a young man from the cast of the Broadway show "Barnum" who, after attending the Beginners' Service, went on to pursue Jewish studies in a yeshiva in Israel.

According to Rabbi Buchwald, from the moment that the *New York Times* story appeared, it became standing room only at the Beginners' Service. Rabbi Buchwald insisted on limiting the number of participants to fifty so that he could relate to each person as an individual. Nevertheless, he pointed out that:

> There were always a few extra chairs on the side for others to squeeze in. People would line up outside the door in the halls and sneak in when anyone walked out. It was also an opportunity or an excuse for me to forcibly "graduate" students who were hanging on in the service for too long. Not too many people were turned away, although one of them was Barbra Streisand. She came on a Shabbat of a Beginners Shabbaton. It was our custom then to spend the second half of the service in the main sanctuary. So when she tried to come in, I sent her down to the main shul.

Rabbi Buchwald estimates that in the thirty years that the Beginners Service has been in operation (he still runs it to this day), he has met and become acquainted with over ten thousand people! And he still limits the seating to fifty people.

> [A bigger place] doesn't work. You have to know everybody, you have to be able to invite everybody [to your home], have a personal relation[ship] with everybody…. Outreach takes place on a personal basis. That's it.

First graduating class of LSS Hebrew School, 1970. First row, middle three:
Rabbi Hershel Cohen, *z"l*, Rabbi Riskin, Cantor Sherwood Goffin.
Credit: Lenore Brown.

In order to fully grasp the impact of the Beginners Service and its revolutionary quality, it is necessary to note how out of place such a service would have been in 1975 within the context of any synagogue, certainly an Orthodox one. The very existence of a Beginners Service presumed that there were Jews who were interested in learning how to participate in the regular prayer service. This was by no means a correct assumption in the synagogue/temple world of 1975. In most synagogue services, the rabbi and the cantor would do all the work while the congregants sat passively in their seats as spectators waiting to be inspired.[8]

Lincoln Square Hebrew School

The different forms of outreach at Lincoln Square attracted hundreds, if not thousands, of people to the synagogue, and there were many programs and courses in place to accommodate those who entered the synagogue through one portal or another. Often, the adults who were drawn in to Lincoln Square expressed a desire to educate their young children within the synagogue. While Rabbi Riskin strongly encouraged people to send their children to a Jewish day school – most frequently to the West Side's Manhattan Day School – not all parents felt ready for such a full-time commitment. To address this need, the Lincoln Square Hebrew School was established within the synagogue in September 1965.

The Lincoln Square Hebrew School offered afternoon classes to children from non-observant homes and, like everything else at LSS, bore its

---

[8] I experienced this many times in my own rabbinate. A congregant would approach me after the service and say, "You know, Rabbi, the service today just didn't inspire me." The first few times I heard this, I felt guilty; I had somehow not done enough to move this person spiritually. Only after a while did it occur to me that although it may have been true that I was not inspiring this individual on a personal level, it did not enter my congregant's head that perhaps there was something that *he* had to do independently in order to encourage inspiration – to learn the meaning of the prayers, improve his Hebrew, concentrate more, and so on. Rabbi Riskin set the bar high regarding expectations of individual self-improvement and encouraged his spiritual staff at LSS to expect the same.

own distinctive stamp. Its principal and administrator was Cantor Sherwood Goffin, who, although not formally trained as a school administrator, offered far more to the parents, teachers, and students than would a typical administrator. Cantor Goffin's easygoing manner, intense spirituality, and musical talent brought a quality of joy and holiness to the atmosphere of the school. These positive qualities were noticeably absent in the vast majority of afternoon Hebrew Schools (and Jewish day schools, too) at that time, and were especially missing in Orthodox Hebrew schools, which carried the reputation – often well-deserved – of having, at best, a boring curriculum taught by incompetent teachers. What the teachers in the Lincoln Square Hebrew School[9] lacked in experience they made up for in their dedication to reproducing for the children the mood, tone, and ambiance that had uplifted Lincoln Square Synagogue under Rabbi Riskin.[10]

In 1971, Rabbi Riskin introduced an innovation at the Hebrew School which was also rare, if not unheard of, in the 1960s and 1970s. He insisted that the school host a Shabbaton several times during the year – a Friday night meal at the synagogue – for the Hebrew school students and their parents. The rabbi felt that it was meaningless to teach children from non-observant homes about Shabbat observance unless there was some way that their families could observe and experience at least one part of Shabbat together. In those days, Hebrew schools would typically teach about the Shabbat laws and rituals only to have the children go home at the end of the day and ask their parents why they were not observing these laws and rituals in their own home. Such innocent questions from the children would often

---

[9] The author was one of them.

[10] Over the years, as I taught and counseled hundreds of university students and adults, the most frequently repeated statement that I heard regarding their Jewish identity was "how Hebrew school had turned them off." When I asked for details, the most common point was expressed as, "We were taught to read Hebrew but we had no idea what we were reading, especially when it came to the prayers." Only after hearing these testimonies did I realize how important the breakthrough of experiential Judaism was at Lincoln Square Hebrew School.

result in a quarrel, sometimes minor, sometimes more intense, which could not easily be resolved.

The Shabbaton experience at the Hebrew School gave families the opportunity to enjoy Shabbat together. Sometimes the enjoyment was so great and the words spoken at the Shabbaton (often by Rabbi Riskin) were so meaningful that some parents began to include aspects of Shabbat observance in their own homes on a regular basis. Several of the students of the Hebrew School, which boasted an enrollment of approximately one hundred students at its peak, went on to become informed, observant Jews.

The Jews of the Soviet Union

In Rabbi Riskin's view, as important as it was to reach out to Jews in order to bring them into the synagogue, it was of equal, if not greater, importance to encourage his congregants, once they were in the synagogue, to go out into the world and put into practice the Jewish ideals of compassion and caring that permeated the atmosphere at Lincoln Square Synagogue. The study programs at the synagogue were successful beyond belief, and the prayer services at Lincoln Square were deeply moving and meaningful, but Rabbi Riskin recognized that Judaism was not just about study and prayer; it was about action, reaching out to people in need. And, in 1964, it was becoming increasingly obvious that there was a group in desperate need of help – the Jews of the Soviet Union.

The Soviet Union's three million Jews had been deprived for decades of almost all expression of their Judaism. The vast majority of synagogues had been closed down, and Jews were severely discriminated against economically and socially. If matters had continued this way, in just another generation there would have been virtually nobody in the USSR who could identify themselves as Jews.

It must be understood that while the Jews of America in 1964 became very involved in the civil rights movement, they were not activists for Jewish causes. As journalist Yossi Klein Halevi, a historian of the Soviet Jewry movement, points out:

The Menorah March for Soviet Jews, Chanukah 1965. L to R: Jacob Birnbaum, founder of SSSJ; Rabbi Riskin, Cantor Sherwood Goffin. Credit: Yaakov and Freda Birnbaum.

Interfaith fast for Soviet Jews, June 1964. Second from right: Rabbi Riskin.
Credit: Yaakov and Freda Birnbaum.

American Jews tended to view the [Soviet Jewry] problem with the same detached paralysis that they had felt during previous periods of trial: There was, after all, no precedent for an effective protest campaign against an anti-Semitic regime.[11]

Jacob Birnbaum, a British Jew living in New York, started the machinery that put an end to the indifference. In 1964 – just months before Rabbi Riskin assumed leadership of Lincoln Square – Birnbaum founded the Student Struggle for Soviet Jewry (SSSJ), the grassroots organization which would ultimately be cited as the catalyst for liberating the Jews from the Soviet Union. Through large-scale rallies, protests, concerts, and the distribution of information sheets, SSSJ was responsible for creating awareness among the American public about the plight of Soviet Jews, and ultimately achieved what seemed impossible – they influenced the Soviet government to change its policies regarding the rights of Jews in Russia, and the rights of Soviet Jews to leave the country, if they so desired.

When Jacob looked for someone to appoint as the chairman of SSSJ, he sought a person who not only could speak charismatically and articulately about the plight of Soviet Jews, but who could help young Jewish Americans feel a strong sense of Jewish identity that would enable them to reach out and identify with the Soviet Jews. Jacob Birnbaum chose Rabbi Steven Riskin for that position. Jacob recalls:

I first got to know [Rabbi Riskin] on his first stay in Israel in 1960–61, and we often discussed *Klal Yisroel* issues [that related to the Jewish people]. Though this was before his *semicha* [rabbinic ordination], already he acted very much like the rav he was later to become in his relation to others. His Seminar kids were among my most committed activists. I recall on a couple of occasions their discussing him in the following fashion: "Yesterday he jumped X number of inches off the ground in his enthusiasm. The previous day, he jumped X+ inches!"[12]

---

[11] Yossi Klein Halevi, "Jacob Birnbaum and the Struggle for Soviet Jewry," *Azure* 17 (Spring 2004).

[12] Written communication from Yaakov Birnbaum to the author, "Rabbi Riskin's Role in the Rise of the Soviet Jewry Movement," May 22, 2007.

Stevie Wonder, they called him. I made him the first chairman of SSSJ.[13]

Yossi Klein Halevi explains that SSSJ under Rabbi Riskin's chairmanship fulfilled one of Jacob Birnbaum's most ambitious goals:

> SSSJ would save not only Soviet Jewry, but American Jewry – by kindling the Jewish passion of its youth. Even as many adult Jews bemoaned the wide-spread involvement of Jewish youth in non-Jewish causes, Birnbaum argued that the real fault lay with the Jewish community, which had failed to offer them an idealistic option. His antidote was the cause of Soviet Jewry.

While the chairmanship was largely honorary, the goal of saving Soviet Jewry became part and parcel of Rabbi Riskin's persona in Lincoln Square and outside it. The cause was constantly mentioned in sermons and classes, where comparisons were frequently made between the slavery of the Jews in Egypt and the suffering of the Jews in Russia. Rabbi Riskin predicted that the Soviet Jews would ultimately celebrate a redemption that would be similar to the Jewish deliverance from Egyptian slavery marked on Passover. SSSJ rallies were announced from the pulpit and congregants were urged to attend. Rabbi Riskin himself often spoke passionately and dramatically at the rallies and marches. Although statistics are lacking, many individual Jews, until that point apathetic and uninformed about Jewish matters, were drawn into the synagogue, propelled by Rabbi Riskin's active involvement in saving Soviet Jewry.

Rabbi Riskin reflects on the by-product of the Soviet Jewry movement – the awakening of American Jews:

> This was a tremendous way of strengthening Jewish nationalism. Letting us understand that we're all responsible, one for the other, and the more Jews can feel the unity of Jews throughout the world, the closer this would bring them to Torah.

---

[13] Jonathan Mark, "Yakov Birnbaum's Freedom Ride." *The Jewish Week,* April 30, 2004.

Rabbi Riskin Travels to the Soviet Union

It was clear to all that Rabbi Riskin was successful in communicating to American Jews the importance of saving Soviet Jewry, but in 1971 the rabbi was called upon to help the Jews in Russia in a much more concrete and direct way. Rabbi Riskin received a phone call one day from the Lubavitcher Rebbe's office asking him to come to a meeting with the Rebbe. At that meeting, the Rebbe asked Rabbi Riskin to go to the Soviet Union to establish four underground *yeshivot* there – in Moscow, Leningrad, Riga, and Vilna. When the rabbi agreed, the Rebbe also put him in touch with the Israel Foreign Ministry, which asked him to open *ulpanim*, Hebrew language schools, in each of these locations.

So, in August, 1971, on the eve of the opening of the new Lincoln Square building on Amsterdam Avenue, Rabbi Riskin traveled to the Soviet Union with two associates. In addition to performing the tasks assigned to him by the Rebbe and the Israeli government, Rabbi Riskin wanted to get a sense of the status and the accomplishments of the refusenik movement. His ability to do this was aided by a young man who approached him at his hotel in Moscow, introduced himself as Leonid Rigerman, and invited the rabbi to his thirtieth birthday party which was taking place at his home. Sensing that this was more than just a birthday party, Rabbi Riskin agreed to accompany Leonid Rigerman to his home, where he found about fifteen people who were willing to talk about the still nascent refusenik movement. Rabbi Riskin and his two associates courageously taped the meeting, and the guests spoke openly of the refuseniks' activities and their passionate desire to leave the Soviet Union and live as Jews.

At that clandestine meeting, Leonid Rigerman told Rabbi Riskin about himself and his family. His Russian-born father and American-born mother lived in New York once they married, but as firm believers of the Communist ideology, they emigrated to Russia from the United States in 1940. Leonid was born in 1940 and raised in Moscow, and since they only spoke English at home, he grew up fluent in both Russian and English. Most important, because his mother was an American citizen, Leonid automatically had American citizenship as well, even though he grew up in Moscow.

Until this day, Rabbi Riskin loves to tell, over and over, the quasi-mystical story of Leonid's reconnection with his Jewish heritage. In 1970, Leonid was in a Ph.D. program in physics at Moscow's prestigious Karpov Institute and at the same time worked in a physics laboratory. Because he spoke and read English, Leonid had been co-opted by the fledgling refusenik movement to do some research for them on international law in the Central Library of Moscow. At that point, Leonid did not really identify with the movement, but he was still willing to do the research.

Sitting in the library one spring day, he came across a copy of the Bible. Never having read it, he flipped through the pages, and came across the story of Joseph and his brothers. His eyes focused on the verse in Genesis 37:17 in which Joseph responds to the question asked of him by the man in the field, "Where are you going?" Somehow, Joseph's answer, "I am seeking my brothers," entranced Leonid Rigerman. The line kept ringing in his ears as he left the library and walked home, passing by Moscow's Great Synagogue. As he approached the synagogue, he saw a line of people waiting. He was told by one of the people standing on line that tonight was the Passover Seder, and they were waiting for the meager distribution of *matza* which the governmental authorities grudgingly permitted in order to avoid the accusation that they were preventing religious observance. Curious, Leonid joined the line, received some *matza,* took it home and ate it. The next day, when he arrived at the physics lab where he worked, he was called to the administrator's office and summarily dismissed from the program. It seems that the KGB had photographed everyone in the *matza* line, and, since he was one of the few young people in that line, he was singled out for punishment. And so it was that Leonid Rigerman became a full-fledged member of the refusenik movement.

One of Rabbi Riskin's associates on this fateful trip managed to smuggle the tape recording of the "birthday party" back to the United States, taped to his chest, but not without Rabbi Riskin's assistance in a cloak-and-dagger operation. The rabbi had been given a Torah scroll in Leningrad by an old

Jew who had hidden and guarded it throughout the Holocaust and in Soviet Russia. He referred to the Torah scroll as "his best friend," and begged Rabbi Riskin to take it out of Russia. At the airport, when the rabbi saw that they were beginning to search his friend who had taped the recording to his chest, Rabbi Riskin created a diversion by screaming at the Soviet officers who were checking his belongings not to touch the Torah scroll. The officers were so busy trying to quiet down Rabbi Riskin, that they allowed his associate to board the plane with the tape still in place. However, the rabbi may have overplayed his part somewhat, because the officers consequently refused to let him on the plane with the Torah scroll. He refused to be separated from it and was taken to a Moscow jail for the night, where he suffered merciless interrogations and terrible conditions. The following day, on account of his American citizenship, the rabbi was transferred to the American consulate in Moscow. He flew back to New York three or four days later, with the promise that the Torah scroll would follow in a diplomatic pouch. The Torah scroll did indeed arrive three months later and was deposited in the Holy Ark at Lincoln Square Synagogue. The tape recording also arrived safely, played (and translated by Rabbi Riskin from the Yiddish) at Lincoln Square, and was forwarded to Senator Henry Jackson, who was instrumental in the US government's actions on behalf of Soviet Jewry.[14]

---

[14] Rabbi Riskin used incidents which took place on this trip to inspire the LSS congregants when he returned. Here is an example: At one point in the trip, Rabbi Riskin was requested to attend a *brit milah* (circumcision), so that he could help the family recite the proper blessings. The *brit* was held at 4 am near a cemetery, so that the KGB would not discover what was taking place. As soon as the *brit* was performed, Rabbi Riskin intoned the traditional prayer, "*Ke-shem she-nichnas la-berit, ken yikanes la-Torah, la-chupah, u-le-ma'asim tovim*" – "Just as he has entered the covenant, may he enter into Torah, the marriage canopy, and good deeds." But after the first word, the baby's father shouted, "*Nein! Nit ke-shem*" – "No, not 'just as!'" The father refused to pray that his son be brought to Torah, the marriage canopy, and good deeds under the same conditions – "just as" – that existed at the time of his *brit*. Rabbi Riskin was deeply moved by the yearning of the Soviet Jews for deliverance, and so were the LSS congregants who heard the story.

At the same time, Rabbi Riskin's other associate on the trip, a bright, ambitious attorney, began to help Leonid Rigerman – long-distance – argue before the Soviet authorities that he should be allowed to leave Russia and travel to the US by virtue of his US citizenship. Although there were some technical procedures which Leonid had to undergo in order to prove his US citizenship, the Russians ultimately authorized his release from the Soviet Union.

Then the fairy tale began. In 1971, Rabbi Riskin invited Leonid (his nickname was Lunya) to come to live at Lincoln Square and to join the synagogue and the community. Leonid accepted the rabbi's offer, taking up residence with the Bergman family, who had an extra room in their apartment. Lincoln Square now had its own personal refusenik! Of course, Lunya was feted and celebrated upon his arrival, invited to members' Shabbat tables, and was asked many questions about the life of the Jews in the Soviet Union. Today Lunya, who has since changed his name to Aryeh, sits in the living room of his Brooklyn home, dressed in Hasidic garb, and reflects:

> [Lincoln Square] was a very warm atmosphere. It was just the right place to start integrating with *Yiddishkeit* [Jewish observance].... Rabbi Riskin gave such a warm *derasha* [sermon].... I've never seen it after that, in no *shul*.

And so, Lincoln Square Synagogue were fortunate to have in their midst a hero of the Russian Jews, who was a living – and English-speaking – symbol of what Jewish activism could accomplish. Lincoln Square members watched Lunya grow in Jewish observance as he attended classes at the Joseph Shapiro Academy. Aryeh Rigerman still speaks to this day of Rabbi Riskin having been the "spiritual center" of the Soviet Jewry movement.

> Rabbi Riskin, I really have great respect and admiration for, because he understood the whole issue. He understood the issue and he understood these are our brothers. It's not [just] somebody who is there [in Russia]. This [the Russian Jews] is part of *kelal Yisrael* [the

Jewish people] and we are *mechuyav* [required] to do anything at all that's possible and he was a spiritual voice of Soviet Jewry.

If Lincoln Square Synagogue needed any further proof of the absolute necessity of breaking barriers, of reaching out beyond the synagogue's walls, even beyond the neighborhood and across the sea to Moscow, Leningrad, Riga and Vilna, Lunya Rigerman was it. What Rabbi Riskin had achieved until then with texts, sermons, and classes, he had now done with human drama. Perhaps equally as important for his congregant students, the concepts of slavery, redemption, and God's eternal promise to the Jewish people had taken on a stark reality that had been missing until that point. This was outreach at its most dramatic; this was Judaism in its most genuine form. Rabbi Riskin, leading the team of groundbreaking educators at Lincoln Square Synagogue, broke down the barriers of the synagogue and moved outside it in order to inspire Jewish people with the Torah.

Rabbi Riskin teaching at Lincoln Square Synagogue, 1975.
Credit: Manhattan Hebrew High School Brochure.

GOD AS A GUEST IN THE SYNAGOGUE

DEUS EX MACHINA is a Latin term that literally means "a god from a machine." In Greek drama, a god was often lowered onto the stage by a crane-like device, the *machina*, in order to rescue the hero or resolve a complicated plot. The term, often used pejoratively, now refers to a play or a novel in which an artificial device or coincidence is used in order to bring about a convenient yet unrealistic solution to a plot.

The Greek dramatists demonstrated brilliance in conceiving this device. After repeatedly witnessing the descent of the gods, the audience would be forced to acknowledge their omnipresence. Furthermore, when a god was lowered to tidy up the messes caused by humans, the public would absorb the idea that the gods do not merely remain in their haven on Mount Olympus but, when necessary, intervene in human events.

The Jewish concept of the divine obviously cannot be compared to the Greek deities, yet, when we consider the state of Judaism in the 1960, we cannot help but notice the absence of the *machina* from the stage upon which the Jewish drama played. Although the search for spirituality was a common motif in the 1960s, many mainstream Jews chose to distance themselves from any quest that would lead to a more meaningful relationship with God and thereby allow Him into their daily lives.[1]

---

[1] As discussed previously, the exceptions were the Havurah movement, which introduced change into conventional synagogue life, and Rabbi Shlomo Carlebach, who revolutionized Jewish music and brought many disaffected Jews back to

While it is true that Abraham Joshua Heschel, whom many considered as one of the most important Jewish theologians of the twentieth century, had written deeply moving theological treatises about the Divine, these seminal works were not being filtered down to the Jewish people's rank and file. While it was true that Rabbi Soloveitchik revealed the beauty of Jewish law and its creative force in his work *Halachic Man* in 1944, it was only in 1983 – almost forty years later – that this brilliant and seminal essay became accessible in English.

When Rabbi Riskin became rabbi of Lincoln Square Synagogue, his objective was to instill in his congregants the same deep love and appreciation of God that was so powerfully instilled in him by his own *Rebbe*, Rav Soloveitchik. Rabbi Soloveitchik's profound connection to God can be clearly seen in his essay about the holiday of Simchat Torah, in which he offered the following interpretation for the ritual of encircling the synagogue while holding the Sefer Torah (Torah scroll):

> ... What is the significance of the *sifrei Torah* [the Torah scrolls] encircling an empty center [of the synagogue on the Simchat Torah holiday]?
>
> The answer is that the center is not empty. God is symbolically there. When nobody is there, Someone is there. There is no place bereft of His Presence. The encircling *sifrei Torah* pay homage to their Divine Author, acknowledging that the purpose of Torah is to direct us to God.

With all of the many functions he performed at the synagogue, Rabbi Steven Riskin never took his eyes off the center of that circle for one moment, and encouraged his congregants to keep their eyes focused there. Members of other traditional Orthodox synagogues at that time, who were used to be being exhorted by their rabbis to observe Jewish law, might have felt jaded and cynical about being told to "experience God." However, the

---

Judaism. However, neither the Havurot nor Rabbi Carlebach operated in the mainstream.

members of Lincoln Square Synagogue were receptive to Rabbi Riskin's attempts to bring God into the synagogue because he avoided a common pitfall that many rabbis of that time fell into – talking about God who was distant from humanity. When his congregants and students speak of Rabbi Riskin's "charisma," and marvel at his power to inspire, they are really taking note of his ability to shed light on the center of that circle and bring God into the synagogue.

Restoring Mystery to Religion

Rabbi Riskin believed that if taught and studied correctly, the Torah provided the key to comprehending the many aspects of God's "personality," and as a result, one could experience God on a personal level. Paradoxically, in addition to encouraging his congregation to approach God as a Friend, Rabbi Riskin also attempted to restore a sense of mystery to religion in general and to Judaism in particular.

Robert Wuthnow, in his description of the state of spirituality in America, describes the change in spirituality from the 1950s to the 1960s:

> Although the 1960s was an unusual decade, filled with radical ideas and shocking behavior, it corrected some of the aberrations that the previous decade had brought to spirituality. The clinging to safe, respectable houses of worship in which a domesticated God could be counted on to provide reassurance was being challenged by religious movements that reasserted *some of the mystery that had always been part of conceptions of the sacred.* [emphasis mine].[2]

Rabbi Riskin made frequent reference in his classes and sermons to the concept of the *mysterium tremendum,* the phrase coined by Rudolf Otto in his seminal work, *The Idea of the Holy*. Rabbi Riskin explained that Otto was expressing the sense of the numinous, that God was "wholly other," a Being

---

[2] Robert Wuthnow, *After Heaven: Spirituality in America Since the 1950s*. Berkeley: University of California Press, 1998, 57.

unlike any that we know and whom we therefore perceive with a sense of deep awe, and even terror and dread.[3]

By introducing to his Lincoln Square congregants concepts from one of the most successful German theological books of the twentieth century, Rabbi Riskin managed to broaden and deepen his students' conception and appreciation of God. For the first time in their lives, the Lincoln Square congregants were studying Judaism and hearing about God and holiness on an intellectual level, backed up by serious sources, both Jewish and non-Jewish.[4]

This was not to say that Rabbi Riskin was not the Great Popularizer – he was. As has been discussed regarding the thought of Rabbi Soloveitchik, Rabbi Riskin had the ability to choose and emphasize the salient points of a particular philosophy and make them easy to understand.

Chassidic Tales

Even if someone could not or did not wish to relate to Rudolf Otto's idea of the Holy, Rabbi Riskin always made sure that his congregants understood that there were many ways to experience God. Although he was a consummate intellectual, Rabbi Riskin realized that people used a variety of paths in order to reach the Holy. To that end, the rabbi filled his sermons and classes with brief stories from Chasidic lore.

---

[3] It is interesting that in Otto's book, the complete phrase is *"mysterium tremendum et fascinans,"* perhaps translatable as "a fearful and fascinating mystery." The full phrase adds the paradoxical point that although God, as a wholly other Being, inspires terror and dread, that "otherness" carries with it a potent charm and attractiveness despite the fear and terror. Rabbi Riskin's emphasis on *mysterium tremendum*, of course, emphasizes the point that the "otherness," the mystery, is really what inspires the fascination.

[4] I believe that Rabbi Riskin may have been the first Orthodox congregational rabbi to quote freely from non-Jewish sources when illustrating religious points, especially important ones like holiness, in Judaism. The door to this approach must certainly have been opened for Rabbi Riskin by Rabbi Soloveitchik, who did the same thing.

He would often relate the question that was asked of the Kotzker Rebbe, the early nineteenth-century Chassidic master, "Where is God?" Rabbi Riskin would intone the Kotzker's answer slowly and with great import: "Wherever you let Him in." Since the Chassidic stories were generally simple tales with a profound message, they could convey spirituality without necessarily demanding the academic or intellectual effort that more formal Torah study required.

It is interesting to note that the Chassidic movement was originally born out of a desire among Jews for a spiritual alternative to the more staid and traditional modes of Torah study.

Professor of Comparative Literature Arnold J. Band points out that:

> [The telling of tales] was regarded as a worthy pastime by Hasidic masters for a variety of reasons: *Since God was immanent in this world* [emphasis mine], he could be present even in a seemingly idle tale which, upon examination, might contain a deep theological truth; the tale projected before the devout the image of the Hasidic hero, the zadik [sic].... [T]he tale was an effective means of communicating basic religious notions.[5]

That being said, it must be understood how rare it was in those days for a Modern Orthodox, Yeshiva University-trained rabbi to be telling Chassidic tales from the pulpit. That is not to say that rabbis of Rabbi Riskin's background did not occasionally insert a Chasidic story into a sermon, but not as a matter of course, and usually not for the purpose of conveying powerful spiritual messages. It was obvious from the sheer numbers of Chassidic stories that he told and his comfort with describing the various Chassidic rabbinic dynasties that Rabbi Riskin had studied Chassidism and had pondered the Chassidic experience. He was clearly not just plucking stories out of context. Rather, he was attempting to infuse the qualities that were part of the Chassidic tradition – spirituality and joy – into a more mainstream form of Modern Orthodoxy. Certain aspects of the Chassidic tradition had already been incorporated into mainstream synagogues, such as

---

[5] Arnold J. Band, *Nahman of Bratslav: The Tales,* New York: Paulist Press, 1978, 30.

the practice of communal singing during the synagogue service. However, Rabbi Riskin was distinct in his use of the Chassidic tale in order to demonstrate God's immanence in this world.

One of Rabbi Riskin's favorite contemporary tales, which he told in the style of a Chassidic story, was about a young boy from a non-observant home who spent a week with his observant grandparents while his parents were away. During that week, he watched his grandmother light Shabbat candles on Shabbat, he saw his grandfather don *tefillin* (phylacteries, or black boxes in which sections of the Torah are written, are worn by observant Jews each weekday), and he saw both of his grandparents kiss the *mezuzah* (a small enclosure containing sections from the Torah) which was affixed to the doorpost each time they entered or left a room. When his parents came to pick him up at the end of the week, they said to their son, "It's time to say goodbye to Grandma and Grandpa. Give them each a kiss." The young boy kissed his grandmother and grandfather, then reached up, kissed the *mezuzah*, and said, "Goodbye, God, I'm going home now."[6]

This story, which Rabbi Riskin repeated to his congregants on many different occasions, including at the end of the Yom Kippur service, reveals, first and foremost, a powerful ability to enter the mindset of the individual who has experienced an intense Jewish experience but must now depart from it. When Rabbi Riskin related Chassidic tales, he was so emotionally involved in what he was saying that it was almost as if his identity was being defined by the story. Professor Band, referring to Nathan of Nemirow's Introduction to *Sippurei ha-ma'asiyot*, a collection of the tales of Rav Nahman of Bratslav, wrote:

> Nathan… realizes that much of the impact of the stories was due to the charisma of the storyteller, Rav Nahman. "It should be clear to any intelligent person that he who hears statements from the very mouth of the sage is not like he who sees them in a book, especially in

---

[6] I do not know the origin of this story, but I first heard Rabbi Riskin tell it at Torah Leadership Seminar in August 1961, on the final night of Seminar. As high school youth who were returning to our homes and communities after a week of intense and enjoyable Judaism, we were weeping uncontrollably by the end of this story.

such allusory [sic] matters as those which cannot be understood without the movement of limbs and the nodding of the head and the wink of the eye and the inclination of the hand etc."[7]

The story of the young boy conveys on a deeper level, in contemporary terms, the same point that nearly every Chassidic tale makes: *Mitzvot* (commandments) are not rote performances but rather represent an actual encounter with God. Stanley Getzler, one of the early members at Lincoln Square Synagogue who later became president of the synagogue, talks about the connection between observing commandments and connecting with God:

> He [Rabbi Riskin] made me think maybe there is a God. And… more realistically, for me, he gave me a way of life [by teaching me about the commandments]. And he gave us Shabbats, and everything that is so lovely about our religion and so meaningful.

Stanley's honest and heartfelt comment encapsulates Rabbi Riskin's entire message: One must meet God, one must be introduced to God, and one must be taught to entertain the notion of a God in this physical world. Encountering the Divine, however, cannot be achieved by philosophical pondering. One can only meet God by performing His *mitzvot*. Shabbat and its laws, the holidays and their observances, the prayers. These commandments all provided Rabbi Riskin with the opportunity to communicate with his congregation on a spiritual level and to bring them into an encounter with God.

---

[7] Band, *Nahman of Bratslav,* 31–32. Whenever I recall a story told by Rabbi Riskin, I recall not only the story but almost the exact tone and inflection with which he told it. Also, when I repeat the story verbally, I automatically find myself trying to reproduce it aurally.

Encountering the Divine

Rabbi Riskin broke the mold of Orthodox rabbis of his time when it came to helping people find God. Robert Wuthnow, a professor of religion at Princeton University, writes about the 1960s:

> The sixties questioned middle-class, white-bread definitions of who God was and of where God could be found, making it more uncertain how to be in touch with the sacred.

When Rabbi Riskin taught his congregants about the *mitzvot* and "how to be in touch with the sacred," he was not inventing new ideas. The teachings could be found in Scripture and in the commentaries, and had existed for centuries. One of the reasons why Rabbi Riskin succeeded was because he was a scholar, and therefore knew in depth what tradition said about the overall purpose of the *mitzvot*. More importantly, though, he never underestimated his congregants. Even though many of them lacked a Jewish background, he did not presume that his congregants were therefore incapable of digesting and absorbing the explanations provided by the commentaries and philosophers. He had a deep, abiding faith that each Jew possessed a spiritual receptor that could accept, understand, and be inspired by a meaningful communication of *ta'amei ha-mitzvot*, a spiritual rationale for the commandments.

Rabbi Riskin, perhaps more than any other Jewish spiritual leader in the 1960s, understood how to tap into the search for spirituality that was prevalent in American society and apply it to Judaism. And so, the sense of the holy pervaded Lincoln Square Synagogue and his congregation of modern Manhattan Jews felt comfortable inviting God there as a welcome guest.

❧ 12 ❦

THE LEGACY[1]

IT SEEMED AS IF IT WOULD LAST FOREVER. Lincoln Square Synagogue's educational outreach programs were steadily growing in attendance and popularity. By the early 1980s, the synagogue had four thousand members, and sixteen hundred people participated in the adult education classes. Rabbi Riskin continued to inspire and motivate his congregants to reach even greater spiritual heights. However, in 1983, Rabbi Riskin informed the Board of Directors of Lincoln Square Synagogue that he would be leaving the synagogue in order to make *aliyah* – move to Israel.

This decision did not come as a shock to the Board. Throughout his career at Lincoln Square Synagogue, Rabbi Riskin had preached about the centrality of Israel to Jewish life, and he had made no secret of his desire to ultimately settle in Israel. In fact, he and his family had spent many summers there in anticipation of their *aliyah*. But the Board of LSS nonetheless insisted that the rabbi's first year in Israel, from 1983 to 1984, be considered a sabbatical. In Rabbi Riskin's mind, however, this first year in Israel would mark the beginning of his family's *aliyah,* their permanent residence in Israel.

By planning his *aliyah*, Rabbi Riskin was continuing a theme that had shaped and defined his rabbinate: he taught by example. Most rabbis of the day – even very Zionistic ones – stopped short of conveying this lesson by personal example; Rabbi Riskin did not permit himself that inconsistency.

---

[1] Since this chapter contains my personal reflections on the legacy of my mentor and *rebbe,* Rabbi Shlomo Riskin, I will be writing in the first person.

LSS farewell to Rabbi Riskin, 1983.
Rabbi dances with Torah scroll presented to him. Credit: Riskin family photo.

Although most of Rabbi Riskin's congregants were not surprised by the announcement, they were perplexed by his timing. How could he leave Lincoln Square Synagogue at the height of his career?

Rabbi Riskin fervently believed that since the ultimate redemption of the Jewish people would arise from Israel, then the preparation for redemption – that is, studying, teaching, and living Torah – should be performed in that country. This was the primary explanation for the decision made by Rabbi Riskin and Vicky to move to Israel at the very height of his career and when he was most influential in the American Jewish community.

Rabbi Riskin frequently taught that the history of the world from a Jewish perspective was not meaningless meandering but rather a linear timeline with a definite direction: Creation, Revelation, Redemption. He stressed that there was a clear starting point and a clear ending point, and that the ending point already stood as a goal at the beginning of the process. The rabbi modeled his life after the sweep of history he so often described. He did not see, as most people do, the timeline of his life proceeding from youth to education to professional accomplishment to retirement. He rather saw his life proceeding more closely along theological lines: he started out his life in the Diaspora, where he educated and inspired Jews, but then moved towards a goal which had, for him, deep theological implications – *aliyah*, a move to the Land of Israel, the primary space for the Jewish People and, thus, the locus of its ultimate redemption.

I believe, though, that there were other factors that contributed to his decision to leave Lincoln Square Synagogue. Shortly after Rabbi Riskin announced that he was leaving LSS for Israel, I took a walk with him from the synagogue up Broadway. I asked him why he was leaving Lincoln Square Synagogue. He seemed momentarily lost in thought and paused for a few moments before talking to me about the many pressures that he faced as rabbi of Lincoln Square Synagogue and what a relief it would be to make a change. Before I had a chance to react, a man rushed up to Rabbi Riskin and said with great urgency, "Rabbi Riskin, Mrs. X is in Mount Sinai hospital. She tried to commit suicide and she needs to see you immediately. I've been trying to contact you. You must go to see her now." As the rabbi turned to find a taxi to the hospital, his brief glance to me spoke volumes and confirmed what he had told me just moments before.

Over the years I have given this incident a great deal of thought and have tried to decode its meaning. Could Rabbi Riskin really have left Lincoln Square Synagogue because he felt pressured by the nature of his work? His entire career had been characterized by extreme demands on his time, but he had never before indicated that he was experiencing difficulties in coping with his harrowing schedule. Relief? His life had always been intertwined with that of his synagogue members – he deeply and genuinely loved and cared about each person there. What could he possibly have meant when he said that he was "relieved" to be leaving? Having been trained by the rabbi always to search for a deeper meaning in the text, the *perush,* I began to reflect further.

It occurred to me that Lincoln Square Synagogue, with all of its talented staff and lay leadership, was the creation of one person and one personality – that of Rabbi Shlomo Riskin. [2] He breathed life into the synagogue, giving it the energy to exist and thrive. When a person becomes a father, he bears responsibility for his child until he or she reaches adulthood. Even though the father is happy to take on that role, he still is burdened by the parental responsibility. The more children parents have, the greater the weight upon them. But what if one "fathers" hundreds, even thousands, of "children"? The joy may be great indeed, but how heavy the weight must be!

Rabbi Riskin would often quote the Rabbinic adage, the commentary to the commandment in Deuteronomy 6:7: "And you shall teach them [the words of Torah] diligently to your *children.*" The Rabbis said, "These are your students, who are always referred to as *children.*"[3] For twenty years, Rabbi Riskin had been responsible for the spiritual welfare of his "children."

I believe that our conversation during our walk on Broadway revealed Rabbi Riskin's inner desire to take the next step with those "children" – to

---

[2] For many years, Rabbi Riskin had wanted to change his name from Steven to Shlomo, but out of deference to his parents-in-law, who had a hard time coming to terms with the Hebrew name, he retained his English name until the late 1970s.
[3] Rashi on that verse, quoting *Sifrei.*

allow them to "grow up" and "leave home" by becoming spiritually independent.

Rabbi Riskin was not simply a rabbi who had devoted twenty years of his life to his congregation. He had taken Jewish neophytes on a twenty-year search for God. He had held their hands in times of joy and tragedy alike. He not only taught, but also opened mind after mind, heart after heart, to a spiritual reality that connected his congregants directly with God and with him. It was hard for both sides to let go. But neither Rabbi Riskin nor his congregation could continue on their own respective journeys unless they embarked on separate paths.

Rabbi Riskin loved to quote the Mishnah in *Avot* (1:1): "Raise up many students." The rabbi explained that although the key Hebrew word in this phrase, *v'he'emidu,* is usually translated as "raise up," the root of the word is *"amod,"* to stand, and the verb in the causative form, *le-ha'amid,* means "to cause to stand." Rabbi Riskin strongly believed that it is a teacher's responsibility to guide and instruct his students in such a way *that they will be able to stand on their own.* While Rabbi Riskin's decision to leave Lincoln Square Synagogue was certainly motivated by a burning desire to live and work in Israel, there was more to it than that. The time had come to see whether he had accomplished his true goal as a teacher: could his students, whom he had taught and inspired, rise to the challenge of *ve-he'emidu?* Could they stand on their own? If so, he had fulfilled the task assigned to him by the Mishnah and by thousands of years of Jewish tradition.

Rabbi Riskin's Legacy

Evaluating the legacy of a leader, political or social, is difficult, especially when that leader is still alive and active. In the political and social realms, however, there are at least areas of activity and scales of performance by which to measure the contribution of a leader. In the religious realm, this measurement is more difficult. How can we gauge success in religious leadership terms – by the number of adherents, the propounding of a new theology? How can one measure the effect of an ideology on people's thinking or lifestyles?

Rabbi Riskin's own words on his legacy are few. He seems strangely uncomfortable discussing the topic. In contradistinction to his larger-than-life pulpit personality and his very friendly and personable manner in small groups or on a one-to-one basis, he is much more reticent when discussing his own achievements. He is aware of how much there is left to accomplish and seems to tacitly define discussion about himself as being in the realm of "small talk," an activity in which he rarely engages.[4]

It therefore seems wise, when trying to identify and evaluate Rabbi Riskin's accomplishments and legacy, to listen to those currently in the best position to sense the short and long-term impact of his work. Included in this category are rabbis who were trained by Rabbi Riskin, other Modern Orthodox rabbis in the field, and heads of yeshivot which try to encapsulate the spirit of Modern Orthodoxy.

Rabbi Ephraim Buchwald

The first person who immediately comes to mind when considering Rabbi Riskin's legacy is Rabbi Ephraim Buchwald. As has been discussed in these pages, for many years Rabbi Buchwald directed the educational programs at Lincoln Square Synagogue, oversaw the Joseph Shapiro Institute, and established the Beginners Service. In addition, he conceived the idea of "Turn Friday night into Shabbos," a bi-annual Shabbat dinner at the synagogue for the entire congregation, and the unaffiliated as well. The credentials he gained at Lincoln Square transformed him into one of the most outstanding rabbis in the field of outreach.

---

[4] This is not a new aspect of Rabbi Riskin's personality. My mother prepared a small celebration for him in our home for his thirtieth birthday at the height of his accomplishments at Lincoln Square. While I think he might even have been embarrassed by the party, he seemed most uncomfortable when I said to him, quietly, during the party, how amazing it was that he had already accomplished so much by the age of thirty. "There's so much left to do," he said.

Rabbi Buchwald recalls a conversation with Rabbi Riskin in the early 1980s, after the success of Lincoln Square Synagogue had already been widely recognized. Rabbi Buchwald asked Rabbi Riskin to help him think of ways they could "go national" with Lincoln Square in order to try to replicate the synagogue's singular achievements throughout the country. Rabbi Buchwald recalls that Rabbi Riskin was very sympathetic to the idea, but says that, "Rabbi Riskin's mind was already on aliyah," his impending move to Israel.

Rabbi Buchwald realized that if he really wanted to perform his outreach efforts on a wider scale, he would have to make it happen himself. So he founded the National Jewish Outreach Program (NJOP) which, over the years, has developed into one of the most successful and well-funded Jewish outreach programs in America. The program features a new iteration of "Turn Friday Night into Shabbat" called "Shabbat Across America," and two core courses are taught throughout the country – "Read Hebrew America," which is a crash course in the Hebrew language, and a "Crash Course in Basic Judaism." Both courses are modeled after classes given in Lincoln Square's Joseph Shapiro Academy. In addition, Rabbi Buchwald has packaged the elements of the Beginner's Service and distributed a curriculum for the service to hundreds of synagogues in the United States.

Rabbi Ephraim Buchwald sees all of the activities of NJOP as an extension of Rabbi Riskin's accomplishments at Lincoln Square:

> [NJOP] is the next step. Really it's taking Lincoln Square synagogue and the programs, replicating it throughout the country, and that's really what we've managed to contribute to, to a very, very needy Jewish community in America.... The Beginner's Service is being replicated in 250 locations. The crash course in Hebrew reading was developed there [at LSS], the crash course in basic Judaism was [also developed there].... We operate in about 3,300 synagogues just in North America.

The founding of NJOP, one of the very first outreach organizations in America, testifies to what Rabbi Buchwald learned from Rabbi Riskin about the primacy of outreach. This organization's efforts to reach out to Jews across the spectrum are a fulfillment of Rabbi Riskin's dream to awaken the spirituality of each and every Jew.

Rabbi Kenneth Brander

For fourteen years (1991–2005), Rabbi Kenneth Brander served as rabbi and developer of the Boca Raton Synagogue in Florida, during which time the community underwent tremendous growth – from sixty to almost six hundred families. Rabbi Brander is currently the Dean of Yeshiva University's Center for the Jewish Future, which was founded in 2005.

The creation of the Center for Jewish Future by Yeshiva University's new president, Richard Joel, and Rabbi Brander's appointment as its dean, signified a renewed commitment from YU to help their rabbis become more effective in the field of outreach. According to Yeshiva University, the Center's goals include developing and supporting rabbis and enriching communities and day schools.

In his fifties, Rabbi Brander is a bundle of energy, known for his seemingly infinite capacity for long hours and hard work. He also has an uncanny way of speaking in pithy phrases, some of which capture the problems of the Modern Orthodox rabbinate and others that point to possibilities for their solution.

Since Rabbi Brander served as the youth director, assistant rabbi, and interim rabbi of Lincoln Square Synagogue, he is in a unique position to comment on Rabbi Riskin's work and to ponder his legacy. Rabbi Brander is proud of his success at the Boca Raton Synagogue, but he is quick to attribute that success to the lessons he learned from his mentor, Rabbi Riskin:

> What Rabbi Riskin was able to do was… to make the synagogue a *haven* and a *heaven* for people. [The *haven* was] a place that protected them, that allowed them to rethink the way they embraced society, and a place that gave them the energy to embrace society in a very creative way. The *haven* part was that you felt a certain warm embrace because you had all these different individuals with different backgrounds finding some form of a cocoon in the institution. The

heaven part was teaching them that religion was more than just the prayer experience. It was an intellectual rendezvous with God. It was a social action piece. And even those who didn't attend – you got the message when you got the mailings.

But what was scalable about Lincoln Square Synagogue? Conceptually, what did Rabbi Brander take away from Lincoln Square that helped him become so successful in Boca Raton?

> When the Boca Raton Synagogue grew from sixty families to over 600 in fifteen years, you're talking about a major growth spurt in a very short period of time…. So you had to *reinvent the synagogue on a regular basis* [emphasis mine]…. Lincoln Square Synagogue… wasn't a "one size fits all" institution…. There were various portals of entry for people to feel connected to the institution…. It wasn't just prayer; it was social action; it was rallies; it was music. It was ways in which people could… gain spiritual flight, spiritual energy, even for those who were not yet connected to engaging in prayer.

Rabbi Brander explains the concept of "portals of entry" to his rabbinical students in the following way:

> [When] I teach the students in rabbinical school now… [I] create a paradigm for what a synagogue is supposed to be…. A synagogue gets its holiness from the *Bet ha-Mikdash* [the ancient Holy Temple which stood in Jerusalem]…. The *Bet ha-Mikdash* was an institution which had various portals of entry, gateways through which people could grow in their relationship with God. It was a place of learning. It was a place of social justice. It was a place where a bride and groom were greeted. It was a place in which a mourner was comforted. It was a place in which there were various spiritual gateways of energy. I think that Rabbi Riskin recognized the fact that, if you want to define a philosophical context for a synagogue, [then you need to] understand its Halachic perspective. And the Halacha of a synagogue is that it's a *mikdash me'at* [a miniature *Bet ha-Mikdash*]…. Rabbi Riskin captured that, whether he saw it in the way I just articulated or not…. When you have those [multiple] gateways, even if you're not a participant in the other gateways, you benefit from that energy.

Rabbi Brander feels that Rabbi Riskin's finely-honed sense of community-building struck at the core of a deeply-rooted twentieth-century problem. In our modern age, with its greater emphasis upon the individual, we have to find new ways to balance the needs of the individual with those of the community. Rabbi Brander believes that Rabbi Riskin addressed this complex issue with sensitivity and finesse as he built the Lincoln Square community. He draws attention to the quality of openness that defined Lincoln Square Synagogue, as Rabbi Riskin attempted to reach out to and accommodate members of the general community. Rabbi Riskin's attitude towards reaching out to Jews on the street – defining them also as "community" – set him apart from other Orthodox rabbis of his day.

Although Rabbi Brander provides a fresh perspective on the goals for Orthodox rabbis and Orthodox communities, it would seem that a quick survey of Orthodox synagogues throughout the United States would show a much greater level of insularity than the model which Rabbi Brander attributes to Rabbi Riskin. It is Rabbi Brander's firm belief that Rabbi Riskin's outlook on outreach should characterize every Orthodox synagogue, and his first priority at the Center for Jewish Future at Yeshiva University is to teach and recreate that model.

> I think that there is... the capacity to make that transformation.... The bottom line is, that's the agenda... when you bring together rabbis in various parts of the country and you teach them, and you start mentoring them effectively....

Rabbi Brander concludes his analysis by citing Rabbi Riskin as the prime example of a rabbi who understood the importance of hiring talented and assertive professionals, which Rabbi Brander feels paved the way for Rabbi Riskin's great success and represents the formula for success in the rabbinate in general.

> Hire people to surround you that are excellent and, even though they may outshine you in certain ways, never be afraid of hiring people who, in some ways, are more talented than you.... I always used Rabbi Riskin as my guiding principle on that. Don't hire people based on

your bar but, basically, hire people who are the best.... [Rabbi Riskin] was never afraid of that. He was never concerned about that, just the opposite. He celebrated that.... He had enough understanding of who he was to basically be willing to hire talented people to surround him who would not be afraid to disagree with him.[5]

Rabbi Kenneth Brander was unquestionably inspired during his years of service at Lincoln Square Synagogue by the community and its distinctive features. There is no doubt that the content, direction, and even some of the programmatic initiatives of his Center for the Jewish Future are fueled by his experience at Lincoln Square, and the professional example set by Rabbi Riskin in the two areas he delineated: the multiple "portals of entry" to the synagogue, and the talented team of educators and spiritual purveyors hired by Rabbi Riskin. Rabbi Brander is absolutely confident that Rabbi Riskin's ideas and innovations will survive and his legacy will inspire others for many generations.

Richard M. Joel

Richard M. Joel assumed the presidency of Yeshiva University in 2003. He is unique in the history of the leadership of that institution in that he is not a rabbi. Rather, with a background in law and academia, he has gained a deep appreciation of the full spectrum of the American Jewish community during his very successful fifteen-year stint as the Director and President of Hillel: The Foundation for Jewish Campus Life. Richard Joel, like his appointee

---

[5] This final point of Rabbi Brander's fits well with Rabbi Riskin's own statement, mentioned above, that he never wanted Lincoln Square Synagogue to become a "cult of personality." Such a point stated by a charismatic figure who was, in fact, the center of Lincoln Square, has to be taken with a grain of salt. However, Rabbi Brander's repeated statements – and similar statements by others – about Rabbi Riskin's management style, especially regarding hiring talented, outspoken people, go a long way toward confirming Rabbi Riskin's claim. Whether this trait was a major ingredient in the success of Lincoln Square and whether it can somehow be embodied in Rabbi Riskin's legacy is left for the reader to decide.

Rabbi Kenneth Brander, offers a superb overview of the picture of Modern Orthodoxy in North America.

As well as an acute observer of the Jewish scene, Joel is responsible for setting policy which will affect Yeshiva University-ordained rabbis, their synagogues, and their communities for years to come. In addition, in his early days, Joel was actively involved in Torah Leadership Seminar and its offshoots and was an intimate friend of Dr. Abraham Stern, founder of Seminar and central figure in the Yeshiva University-centered outreach movement.

Richard Joel attributes Rabbi Riskin's success at Lincoln Square to his Torah Leadership Seminar experience.

> He learned [his approach] at Seminar. He believed that if you found a way to have people see a Torah lifestyle based on substance [at Seminar] and he created a community where they were not alone and where they could be reinforced in it, then it would work… The language I translate it into [is that] for Jewish life to go on… Jewish people have to *know* the story and they have to *own* the story [verbal emphasis his]. It's not just knowledge, it's knowledge and experiential Judaism.

Richard Joel's analysis of the conceptual framework that Rabbi Riskin envisioned sounds obvious until we recall that no one was talking about "experiential Judaism" in the context of the synagogue in the 1960s.[6] As the earlier chapters of this book have demonstrated, Lincoln Square not only fulfilled the traditional function of the synagogue as a place to pray, but also created opportunities for a Jewish experience.

Since Rabbi Riskin's main goal was Jewish education rather than building an impressive synagogue membership list, he introduced countless number of activities, events, and programs so that his congregation could benefit from them both on an individual and communal level.

---

[6] As discussed in Chapter 1, the Havurah movement, which did not begin until 1960, was not founded as part of the synagogue and certainly was not associated with Orthodox Judaism.

[The community aspect was] critical. Because you can't dance around the Shabbat table alone…. [Yet] The work that Shlomo Riskin did was based on establishing I-thou relationships…. He had basic respect for the individual…. He had the warmth to say, "Come into my home."… [He had] that unique combination of both teacher and host.

Richard Joel continues with the following analogy:

When he built the *shul,* it was a community that valued learning and valued Jewish living. [Rabbi Riskin said,] "We're going to put you in a greenhouse, a controlled environment, where we can have you see the passion of Torah. The only other way to get it is living in a Jewish home and growing [up] in a Jewish home and sharing your values with your family…. [In the absence of this, your family is]… Lincoln Square Synagogue."

But Richard Joel does not seem satisfied with the scope of his own analysis. He struggles to place Rabbi Riskin's work in a broader theological context. Joel believes that Rabbi Riskin created an environment in Lincoln Square Synagogue where his congregants could freely explore the covenantal relationship between God and the Jewish people. Rabbi Riskin taught his LSS congregants and students how to uphold their side of the covenant with God. In that sense, Rabbi Riskin made Lincoln Square's real mission a universal one, a prophetic mission that emanates from the covenantal relationship: to be a light unto the nations.

But what was it about Rabbi Riskin's personality that made him so successful?

He understood the disciplined use of charisma…. Charisma is dangerous, it's like fire, so if you contain it, and you put it into something holy, like a *menorah* [a ritual candelabrum], it warms and lights. If you leave it alone, it consumes and burns. [Rabbi Riskin did not say,] "You like me. Look how special I am, look how charismatic I am. I'm going to draw you close, so that the goal should be that you want to be me."

I think what Rabbi Riskin did was, the goal is, "I'm bringing you close so that you can be you."

Rabbi Riskin's greatest strength was, first of all, he was a brilliant man, [and] secondly, he really is *emmesdick* [genuine].

Rabbi Avi Weiss

Rabbi Avi Weiss is the Senior Rabbi at the Hebrew Institute of Riverdale in New York, but has gained prominence as the Founder and President of Yeshivat Chovevei Torah, a recently-established institution for the ordaining of rabbis dedicated to what Rabbi Weiss calls "Open Orthodoxy." This term represents a commitment to the Torah and its commandments while maintaining an openness toward secular culture and thought.

The mission statement for Rabbi Weiss's synagogue could have been written by Rabbi Riskin himself, and is reminiscent of Lincoln Square Synagogue's "Our Credo," written by Rabbi Riskin in 1965:[7]

> [We are an] Orthodox synagogue which serves the entire Jewish community... [which] warmly embraces all Jews regardless of affiliation, commitment or background. [We are] known as the "Bayit," which is home – a place of love and welcome. The Hebrew Institute of Riverdale is known for bringing spirituality into the synagogue, for its activism, its learning programs, and its work on behalf of the elderly, homebound, and the mentally and physically challenged.

Rabbi Weiss openly admits that his career – his very conception of the rabbinate – was deeply influenced by Rabbi Riskin.

> What attracted me was [his] inspiration, the brilliance... I felt his emotion, and I wanted to transmit that emotion.... He was dealing with complex topics... and he was able to say it in language that was deep, articulate, and yet could touch the common folk.... He

---

[7] See Chapter 5 for an in-depth examination of Rabbi Riskin's "Credo."

impacted upon me in many ways. The "Bayit" [Rabbi Weiss' synagogue] is shaped in its own way and Chovevei, too, and so on. But he planted the seeds. He impacted upon me, and he deserves a lot of the credit. And I think he's impacted on a lot of rabbis. He impacted so powerfully. He probably doesn't even know who he's impacted on.

Rabbi Weiss describes Rabbi Riskin as someone who is both intellectual and inspirational.

> Shlomo was effusive. He was inspiring because he was inspired…. He was on fire. Where you were in his presence, he was just overflowing with love of Torah, love of God, love of his fellow person. I don't think you can inspire unless you're inspired. He was on fire. He still is on fire. He was so inspirational… that people often looked down on his intellect. He's brilliant. He is absolutely brilliant.

Finally, Rabbi Weiss observes that Rabbi Riskin showed that it was possible to be deeply committed to Jewish law and practice while at the same time being open and reaching out to the wider Jewish community, something that was previously thought to be paradoxical.

> He is a deeply, deeply religious man. He is [also] meticulously Halachic… meticulous in his halachic observance. *He's not "Orthodox-lite"* [emphasis mine]…. He maintains the concreteness, the anchoredness of Orthodoxy, and yet he's open. He's doing things in a very different way…. He created something very different in Lincoln Square. It was a deflection; it was a change…. He was reaching a broader community.

Can the "Rabbi Riskin phenomenon" be replicated? Rabbi Avi Weiss is not sure:

> I think a Shlomo Riskin comes along once in many, many, many, many, many decades. He's very [sic] unique. And sometimes, leadership, I think some of it you just have to be born with, [but some of it] you can learn…. I can never thank him enough.

Rabbi Edward Davis

Rabbi Edward Davis has been the spiritual leader of the Young Israel of Hollywood-Ft. Lauderdale, Florida, for over twenty-five years. Before that, he served as the rabbi of a congregation in Richmond, Virginia. Over the course of eight years, during college and graduate school at Yeshiva University, Rabbi Davis served as the *ba'al koreh* (Torah reader) at Lincoln Square, when Rabbi Riskin had just arrived at the synagogue. Rabbi Davis, who was single at the time, ate most of his Shabbat meals with the Riskins. As a "permanent guest" at the Riskins' home, he learned a great deal from Rabbi Riskin both by talking with him and, as he puts it, "by osmosis" – through simply observing him in action.

Rabbi Davis, often whimsical about his own emotional restraint, gives credit to Rabbi Riskin for teaching him how to get in touch with his emotional side:

> My Judaism was more cerebral than it was emotional. The Rav [Rabbi Soloveitchik, with whom Rabbi Davis also studied] was all cerebral, certainly not emotional. [With] Rabbi Riskin, you saw the other side, that you could be both. Granted, too much emotion for me, but at least it brought it to another level.

In the early seventies, Rabbi Davis taught Bible and Talmud at Lincoln Square's Joseph Shapiro Institute for adult education. He emphasizes how revolutionary Rabbi Riskin was about serious adult education, to the extent that it shaped the essence of Rabbi Davis' conception of his own rabbinate:

> I place adult education [in my rabbinate] the very top of my list as to what I was going to do, and that was clearly as a result of the [experience]at Shapiro....

Rabbi Davis further illustrates Rabbi Riskin's profound influence on other rabbis and the dissemination of the LSS message:

> Don't forget Lincoln Square was not a national movement. [But] it did give birth to a lot of things: People like us [himself and the author]

were influenced and carried a message – not a message, but carried *that style* [emphasis mine] with us…. Rabbi Riskin showed how to deal with people, how to talk to people…. It's got to be "real meat" in terms of what you're offering. Clearly I learned that from him.

Lincoln Square Synagogue may not have been a "national movement" in the conventional sense. It had no constitution, officers, or national headquarters. However, most serious intellectual and social movements – national and international – did not have those trappings either. The defining feature of such movements is their ability to effect change. By inventing a new "style," as Davis words it, the Lincoln Square phenomenon was on equal footing with other "national movements."

Furthermore, what Rabbi Davis describes as "style" can also be understood as reinventing both educational and leadership theories. Additionally, Rabbi Riskin's insistence upon infusing his teachings with "essence" and "real meat" set a new bar for the Modern Orthodox rabbinate.

Rabbi Shaul Robinson

Scottish-born Rabbi Shaul Robinson, the present rabbi of Lincoln Square Synagogue, speaks with great reverence of Rabbi Riskin, under whom he studied for eight years in Israel. In trying to define his own personal legacy from Rabbi Riskin, he talks about the relationship between a rabbi and his congregation.

The most… fundamental lesson I learned from Rabbi Riskin was that every interaction [of a congregant] with the rabbi, no matter how painful, should be a positive one. The rabbi's there to help you, even if the answer to the question is "no."

The rabbi cares about you, the rabbi has a vision…. It's a question of becoming part of people's lives. I believe that very, very firmly, and I got that straight from Rabbi Riskin.

When considering Rabbi Riskin's impact on Jewish outreach, Rabbi Robinson shares the following insight:

> From everything I understand, it [the outreach idea] started here [at LSS] and it was, A, successful, and, B, *so intuitive that that's what a shul could do* [emphasis mine]. [The legacy] is almost too big…. It changed the way that people think. It's like asking if the spirit of the Enlightenment is still alive. I don't know, [but] we all think differently now [post-Enlightenment], so there's a natural assumption [that the sprit is alive].

Rabbi Shaul Robinson, sitting in the same chair in the same office in which Rabbi Riskin sat for twenty years, speaks matter-of-factly about the metamorphosis of Modern Orthodox Judaism brought about by Rabbi Shlomo Riskin. The understanding that synagogues are for outreach and that rabbis must be part of congregants' lives now pervades the consciousness of Rabbi Riskin's successor, and that of so many of his colleagues and their congregations.

Rabbis Robinson, Brander, Weiss, and Davis – and other Jewish leaders like Richard Joel – have created a "national movement" inspired by Rabbi Riskin's ideas and the way he applied them to Lincoln Square Synagogue. Similarly, their congregants and students have come to expect from their spiritual leaders a deeper approach, a level of substance, a particular type of openness in Jewish leadership that inspires a deeper connection with their own spirituality. Rabbi Riskin's dream and his legacy live on. *Ve-he'emidu* – the students are standing on their own.

A Message of Redemption

In these pages, we have read how a young Brooklyn boy from an extremely secular home became one of the most noted Orthodox rabbis in America in the 1960s. We have followed the spiritual journey of the founders of Lincoln Square Synagogue, a small group of Manhattan Jews whose initial motivation in establishing a synagogue was for the purpose of getting together and socializing. And we have heard the leaders of major institutions for the training of Modern Orthodox rabbis in America testify that almost all of their outreach programs are built upon the ideas and successes of a rabbi who never held an administrative position in any of those institutions.

But before we conclude, I would like to tell one more story that Rabbi Riskin shared with me recently. It is a story from his childhood that will shed some light on the rabbi's abundant supply of spiritual energy and his revolutionary attitudes towards Jewish spirituality and redemption.

It was the summer of 1948, and eight-year-old Steven Riskin had just learned from his rabbi about the upcoming day of Tisha be-Av (the summer fast day that commemorates the destruction of both Temples in Jerusalem, and, in a way, all Jewish tragedy and suffering). Young Steven decided that he would fast on this day and, after morning services, would walk over to his yeshiva and review the tractate of the Talmud that he had studied in class during the past school year. While he was studying in the Yeshiva, a tall, stately man entered the study hall. Rabbi Riskin describes him in the following way:

> He was wearing a black frock coat with a black kippa – a yarmulke, not a hat – and the coat was torn on the right side, which is a sign of mourning for a loss of someone other than a parent (in which case the tear is made on the left side). He sat next to me and put his arm around me. He had a beard and *payot* (sidelocks), which was a rarity in our neighborhood at that time. He said to me, "You know, you're not supposed to study regular Torah on Tisha be-Av, because Torah brings joy to a person's life. This is a day of mourning; let's study something else."

> And he took out the Tractate *Gittin* and he started studying with me. For the first time I heard the story of Kamtza and Bar Kamtza, which is a story illustrating how the Second Temple was destroyed because of baseless hatred between Jews.[8] We must have spent three or four hours learning that whole passage. The time passed very rapidly.

---

[8] The story, found in Tractate *Gittin* 55b of the Babylonian Talmud, tells of a wealthy man who hosts a lavish banquet for his friends in Jerusalem shortly before

Not only were the stories of the Destruction riveting, but he taught them as if he had actually been there. The Talmudic stories, the entire historical period came alive, and we spent what were for me magical hours. Then he kissed me on the forehead and recited the *Birkat Kohanim* (Priestly Blessing) over me. He then said, "With God's help, you'll be a rabbi for the Jewish people." And he quickly left the yeshiva.

Rabbi Riskin concludes this strange story by describing his grandmother's reaction to the incident. After spitting in young Steven's eye in order to ward off the "Evil Eye" (which was uncharacteristic behavior for his normally rational grandmother), she said to him with tears of joy in her eyes, "I believe you met Eliyahu ha-Navi [Elijah the Prophet] and you are going to be a rabbi."

To this day, Rabbi Riskin still asks himself whether he actually met Elijah the Prophet or whether it was just a chance encounter with a very kind Talmud scholar. Whoever the man in the torn coat was, Steven Riskin never saw him again.

Most Jews associate Elijah the Prophet with a mystical figure who, according to tradition, visits every Passover Seder (the special meal of Passover eve, at which a cup of wine is set aside for him). He is there to

---

the destruction of the Second Temple. He tells his servant to invite his best friend, who is called Kamtza, but the servant mistakenly invites a man named Bar Kamtza, who is his employer's worst enemy. At the banquet, when the error is discovered, the host insists upon ejecting Bar Kamtza before all the guests, refusing his offer to pay for the entire meal rather than be publicly humiliated. Prominent rabbis, themselves guests at the banquet, witness the incident but remain silent. Incensed at the rabbis' failure to intercede on his behalf, Bar Kamtza passes false information to the Roman authorities that ultimately results in Rome's decision to sack Jerusalem and destroy the Temple.

It is difficult to judge which of the lessons of this story – the destructive power of baseless hatred, the terrible results of the rabbis' silence in the face of evil, the possibility of horrific consequences stemming from a single vile act – young Steven Riskin absorbed on that Tisha be-Av day. But all of those lessons became themes of his life and his teaching.

promise that complete redemption of the world will eventually follow the Jews' redemption from Egypt. Elijah's name is also invoked and a special chair set aside for him at every *brit milah* (ritual circumcision), which is held to welcome eight-day-old baby boys into the Covenant of Abraham. At a *brit,* Elijah is present to assure us that the covenant between God and the Jewish people will last forever. In the Bible, Elijah is a historical prophetic figure who, according to the prophet Malachi, will introduce the Messiah to the world at its final redemption.

Less known is the phenomenon in the Talmud, the great corpus of Jewish law and thought, of *gilui Eliyahu,* a revelation of Elijah, in which he appears to someone in human form in order to deliver a crucial message or teach a profound lesson for life.

The historical figure of Elijah is a prophetic teacher with his eye on the future. Did young Steven Riskin experience a *gilui Eliyahu,* a visit from Elijah, disguised as a Talmudic scholar? Was there even a man in black at all, or was this story the product of an already creative and searching mind and heart reflecting on the meaning of the day? We will never know. But whoever this mysterious man was, in just a few short hours he instilled in young Steven a deep love for the Torah and the Jewish people and a sense of hope for a bright and redeemed future. He also imparted to Steven the tragedy of the Jewish people and showed him the burning need to heal that tragedy with love and compassion. From that moment on, the mission of Elijah the Prophet and that of Rabbi Shlomo Riskin were one and the same: to educate, to inspire the study of God's word, to reconfirm His Covenant, and to prepare the world for its ultimate redemption.

Epilogue: In the Epicenter

LINCOLN SQUARE SYNAGOGUE was founded and flourished as an American Jewish institution, firmly rooted in the center of the largest city in the United States. Rabbi Riskin was born in Brooklyn to American-born parents and married Victoria Pollins, the descendant of several generations of American-born Jews. English was the vernacular of virtually everyone in the synagogue; American traditions and holidays were noted and respected. On the face of it, everything about Rabbi Riskin and Lincoln Square Synagogue was American.

Yet, as has been discussed in this book, the State of Israel played an active role throughout the synagogue's early years to an extent that was rare in those days (and perhaps is becoming rare again). This role was not only the more typical one of Israel as the recipient of *tzedakah,* the focus of financial appeals for its welfare and stability. Nor was Israel's role in the synagogue relegated to "Israel the museum" – a place to visit in order to see the footsteps of Jewish history.

Rather, the role highlighted two aspects of Israel that were often downplayed in those years: Israel as a place for Jews to live, and Israel as the center of Torah, the locus from which redemption will sprout. Early in his tenure at LSS, Rabbi Riskin arranged with the synagogue leadership that he would spend every summer in Israel studying and living, more or less, as an Israeli. Rabbi Riskin's spoken Hebrew was excellent at a time when this was not common for Orthodox rabbis.

Yet most important was the Israel expressed within the Torah lessons that he constantly preached and taught. When he explained the lyrical proclamation in the Song at the Sea (Exodus 15:2), "This is my God and I will glorify Him," Rabbi Riskin always emphasized the less popular of Rashi's two opinions – and the opinion of Onkelos in the Torah's Aramaic translation – as to *how* the singers planned to glorify God. "I will build Him a home," the rabbi would shout. "The true redemption from Egypt was not complete until they arrived in the Land of Israel – their home and God's home – and built him His Home, the Holy Temple in Jerusalem."

Looking back, it is hard to imagine that not everyone understood, almost from the very beginning, that Manhattan was only a stopover for Rabbi Riskin. A product of New York and America, the rabbi understood how Americans thought and how they built. Yet at the same time, he always turned his eyes eastward, towards home.

As stated above, this book is not about Rabbi Riskin's work in Israel. That would require another entire volume, which would begin with his dream of building Efrat, a kind of model city, in the Gush Etzion region south of Jerusalem. It would detail the triumphs and disappointments along the way, together with the important questions, such as whether the city should be religious only or mixed, thus perhaps becoming another Lincoln Square-style phenomenon – a kind of outreach center, this time based in Israel.

That book would describe the various programs in the Ohr Torah Stone Institutions, Rabbi Riskin's rubric of operations in Israel. It would show readers the rabbi's vision, which includes increased opportunities for women within a strict halachic context, and his pioneering work in creating *toanot rabbaniyot* (rabbinical pleaders), specially-trained women who appear regularly before the rabbinical courts, a precedent-setting phenomenon, to say the least. That work would also describe the rabbi's deep concern for and creative thinking about the *agunah* problem, which keeps women "chained" to husbands who refuse to divorce them. The chronicle of Rabbi Riskin's work in Israel would discuss in detail the latest stage of his vision: the training of rabbis in his special brand of outreach and their placement around the world in influential positions.

The book would reveal Rabbi Riskin's courage in calling for ways to place more Modern Orthodox rabbis and judges in important positions in the Israeli rabbinical structure so that Israeli society would feel more deeply the openness and special non-judgmental character of his approach at Lincoln Square.

But even without an additional volume, it is clear even to the casual observer that Rabbi Riskin feels that he is in the right place. It is obvious that as important as his Lincoln Square years were, they were really the dress rehearsal for the actual performance: his studying, teaching, and reaching out where, ultimately, it really matters: the Land of Israel.

While he was still in New York, Rabbi Riskin said many times, "When Jewish history is written, New York, Johannesburg, and London will be but footnotes to the text. And the text will be the Land of Israel."

Rabbi Riskin knew that this was hard for American Jews – who, like himself, were steeped in American culture – to hear. But as we have seen, part of the rabbi's great talent was to make the great challenges of Judaism – being different, observing sometimes difficult and impenetrable laws – not only palatable, but enjoyable and joyful.

Aliyah, uprooting one's self and moving to Israel, is not easy. It was certainly not easy for Rabbi Riskin and his family. But he did it and preached it, like he did every other *mitzvah*, with verve, purpose and joy. Several members of the Lincoln Square community heeded the call and followed. Virtually all members of the community – and many outside it – were inspired once again by the special, individualistic way that Rabbi Riskin taught a commandment of the Torah – perhaps its most all-encompassing commandment – to change one's locus and focus and start life anew in Israel.

For Rabbi Riskin, text meets life once again. "This is my God, and I will glorify Him." Rabbi Riskin, who built Lincoln Square Synagogue as a prelude, lives and works in Israel, building God His permanent Home.

Rabbi Shomo Riskin was born on May 28, 1940 in Brooklyn, New York. Although his family was not religiously observant, he attended a local Orthodox yeshiva, the Yeshiva of Brooklyn. He graduated from Yeshiva University in 1960 and became an ordained rabbi under the guidance of Rabbi Joseph Soloveitchik.

In 1963, Riskin received his Master's degree in Jewish history, and he completed a Ph.D. from New York University's Near Eastern Languages and Literature department in 1982. From 1963 until 1977, he lectured and served as an Associate Professor of Tanakh and Talmud at Yeshiva University in New York City. He became the founding rabbi of Lincoln Square Synagogue in New York City in 1964 and served in that position until 1983. During the 1960s and 1970s he was an outspoken leader of the movement to allow free, unrestricted emigration for Soviet Jews and made several trips to the USSR in order to visit and encourage the Jewish communities there.

In 1983, Riskin immigrated to Efrat, Israel with his family. There he became the city's rabbi, a position he still retains. He also established the Ohr Torah Stone network of high schools, colleges, graduate programs, seminaries and rabbinical schools, whose total student enrollment numbers in the thousands.

Riskin is the author of several books, including *Women and Jewish Divorce*, *The New Passover Haggadah*, the *Torah Lights* series and *Around the Family Table*, as well as many scholarly articles. He also writes a weekly column on the Torah portion of the week that is published in the *Jerusalem Post* and in dozens of Anglo-Jewish newspapers around the world.

About the Author

Rabbi Edward Abramson received a B.A. in English literature, an M.A. in Jewish history, and *semicha* (rabbinic ordination) from Yeshiva University. He and his mother, Anne, were early members of Lincoln Square Synagogue, where he met his future wife, Miriam. Rabbi Abramson served a congregation in Saratoga Springs, NY from 1973 to 1976, and was the principal of two Jewish day schools in the New York City area. He and his family made aliya to Israel in 1983, where he served as educational director of the World Union of Jewish Students in Arad. Later, he served in the same position at the Pardes Institute of Jewish Studies in Jerusalem.

Rabbi Abramson, who has also pursued business interests in Israel, served as an advisor on North American affairs for the Deputy Foreign Minister of Israel. Through speaking, teaching, and writing, he has reached out to many audiences uninitiated in Torah study, and sees himself as an appreciative beneficiary of the Jewish outreach movement of the 1960s.

Rabbi Abramson and his wife, Miriam, live in Jerusalem. They are the parents of three grown children and the grandparents of four.